MOLLY

The Molly Project

Journey with Molly & the Psalms to Healing

Sept /19

To a dear friend from Medhurst,
Martha you have a lovely heart +
I am so glad we have met!
Blessings to you + may this
book assist you helping others
on their journey !

M . E . D .

Mary Daly
(+ molly too)

ISBN 978-1-64258-261-1 (paperback)
ISBN 978-1-64258-262-8 (digital)

Christian Faith Publishing, Inc.
832 Park Avenue
Meadville, PA 16335
www.christianfaithpublishing.com

Printed in the United States of America

Acknowledgments

This book is a thank offering to many. First, thank you to members of my support team: HGB, MBC, and LAK. You know who you are and that is all that matters to Molly and me. Thank you for journeying with us to the finish line. We all need good friends, and you demonstrated that to me during my healing.

Secondly, thank you to the members of the Molly Project edit team. They include five reviewers before the draft went to the publishers.

Lastly, and most importantly, I thank God as creator, caregiver, and healer. Without God's healing at various intersections in my life journey, I would not be writing this book.

> ### *What is Life?*
>
> *Life is people!*
> *Man was built for communication.*
>
> *He was given arms to reach out*
> *and warm the saddened heart.*
>
> *He was given eyes to see*
> *the beauty of his fellow man.*
>
> *But most importantly,*
> *he was given lips to speak*
> *and ears to hear*
> *the joys and sorrows of his friends.*
>
> *Life therefore is neither money,*
> *nor machine; but rather,*
> *it is learning and growing with others.*
>
> —Written by Molly's adult long before they met

Contents

PHASE FOREVER

Disclaimer

What? A book starting with a disclaimer? Is it worth reading? Yes. **This book will be a valuable resource because it is a story of heart, life, and recovery from sexual abuse through God's work, and patience.** This is the book I wish I had been able to read during the difficult stages of my journey.

1) Theological disclaimer

I do not claim to be an expert in Hebrew poetry whatsoever. I have studied the Psalms at seminary, but that felt introductory at the time as most formal education is before life practice. The book of Psalms is unique in the Bible. Using an English translation and our current understandings, we often fail to see the Psalms with their artistic and lyric beauty. As with many books of poetry, some people appreciate the book of Psalms and others do not. Some will respect the variety of language and emotion, others will not.

Many churches include the reading of a Psalm passage each Sunday, while others leave them out as they are seen to have less value than the New Testament Scriptures. Why? Within many Psalms there is a sense of anger and hatred (usually not seen as a very spiritual trait), and within a few verses this shifts to love and thankfulness. Many of us can relate to the range of emotions found within these poems. The Psalms represent real life emotion which many of us work hard to suppress. For the abused and others struggling with the weight of the world, we have "walked through the valley of the shadow of death" (Psalm 23:4) and we can understand and identify with the span of emotions presented.

Back to my theological disclaimer: while the book of Psalms may be analyzed in its original language and seen from the most intellectual approach, mine is more of a "heart study" of the text. I will not misrepresent God's word, but I use it in the artistic and poetic approach to communicate story and emotion, emotions that we can relate to at an honest level.

2) Counseling disclaimer

I have read many books over my years. I was in a group therapy class at seminary, took counseling classes each semester, and have been to counselors myself. I feel I have significant personal experience to share, but I am not a trained psychologist. I have no credential to cure you except my own life story along with God's direction to help others.

3) Medical knowledge disclaimer

As you will soon discover, I have struggled with the health care system and have avoided it as best I could. I have little to offer in medical or pharmacological advice, but I know it would be best to start any mental health journey in a physician's office. There could be stress being brought about by chemical imbalances and various medical conditions. Your doctor may be able to get a full picture of issues you may face and provide practical solutions. There is, however, no easy pill for curing matters of memories. It will take time to resolve. And prescriptions may either cover symptoms or be helpful with the journey. I encourage you to search for wise medical advice.

4) Legal Disclaimer

I cannot provide best legal practices for the journey that may be needed. Each country has its own rules, and if intervention is needed, seek it out. You will find some information in the Coda section at the end of this book, but this book is a book to assist with personal healing and not the many other important avenues in the journey to help others and oneself.

There, it is out. Four disclaimers that I am not a theology expert or a counseling specialist, nor do I understand everything about the complex interactions of the human body, and neither can I give you any legal advice. That covers mind, heart, and soul for the one needing healing as well as their interactions with the one who has harmed them.

While not an expert in many things, I am an interesting mix of these through education and life experience with a heart to follow God's will and serve in ministry to others who struggle.

The writing of this book is a step of faith to help others and one for which I clearly saw God's leading. I began this project in 2011, had the chapters decided, the journey plotted, the scriptures chosen, and the "M" chapter names completed. There were little bits written in journals, poem logs, all stuffed in a binder to put in later. Here it is five years later. Yikes! Where did that time go? October 2016, I became serious about completing the writing. In faith, I quit my full-time job and set Molly work time each day as though this was my full-time job. I have felt accountable to God to complete the work and more passionate with each passing day to help others who remain lost in the struggle of past traumas.

M.E.D.

This book is one tool in the toolbox of your journey. I pray it is life changing!

Gracious God, may the words I write be of your leading.
Use me to help others learn, grow, and find healing.
Lord may you be glorified. Amen.

Introduction

I take you back to 1996. I was recently settled in a new city with a new life. I had finished my second master's degree, landed a full-time job, and bought a home in a new city. Things were going well. I had arrived, hadn't I? I found a church home, and had a great pet. After eleven years of university it was nice to relax.

I offered to help a mom and her two kids in crisis by letting them stay in my home in their time of need. Who wouldn't in my situation? Paying it forward, a thankfulness for the present success. I had the space for them, and they were there within hours of asking. I was doing the right thing. I could help others, which felt fulfilling.

Within what seemed like a short time, the panic attacks started. **What** was wrong with me? I learned later that being in one's thirties and feeling settled was a common time for victims of sexual abuse to start to remember . . . to be stirred . . . to be triggered because of finally feeling a sense of safety. My, we are a complicated species, aren't we?

The mind is fascinating. How does it manage to filter so many things for us? How does it remember? How does it forget? If you are reading this book, you no doubt have experience with traumatic memories or know someone who is struggling. I am not an expert on the brain, but matters of the heart and the trauma of sexual, physical, and emotional abuse are all (unfortunately) an area of study for me. I am thankful for the magical work of the subconscious in my life. I would not want to have remembered everything from day one as I doubt I could have functioned in life. I also needed some stability in my life to keep a sense of foundation beneath my feet when all seemed to be lost.

This book about Molly and her journey has been stirred within me for many years for the following five reasons:

1) What? An estimated one in four girls/women have been sexually abused or raped! That statistic seems high, but I have read it in many different places. Then there are the boys . . . As this book enters its final editing stage with the publisher, social media and the news have been surprised with a "Me Too" campaign started in October 2017 after Harvey Weinstein was accused of many sexual advances of Hollywood stars. Now there is an epidemic of people sharing their secret shame and giving strength to others to type the two short words into a Facebook Post. This recent movement will help remove the stigma for all of us to share our stories. What are we doing to help these many individuals?

2) Going to a session entitled "Healing the Trauma of Sexual Abuse" and being disappointed it was not given an appropriate title. There was discussion of what abuse is and how victims need to let go and forgive the perpetrator. The speakers said that an inability to forgive the perpetrator is holding the victim back from healing. There was, surprisingly, no discussion of the actual journey, the many hurdles to overcome, or practical tips for healing. The only message given in this presentation was that the abuser needs to know they are forgiven. **What?** This will only come at a very late stage in healing, if indeed ever, but not the start! In fact, many authors whose books I have read said this could be detrimental to the healing process (see chapter 19). My process was to deal with the shame and shock and sort my life out . . . not go to them and forgive them first. They needed forgiveness FROM ME? I don't think so. They need to be honest and not cover up their crime that is true, but that is their process not mine. They need to come to me and apologize.

I had gone to this session to find the tools for recovery but found nothing new in my toolbox when I left. It seemed what was in the security of my healing process had been somehow stolen through the session! I was crying silently. I was as near to the back of the room as I could be, and I noticed others were crying too. I found myself being angry. I left with a feeling of utter disappointment.

3) I am a Christian but have struggled with how the church can be poor in welcoming people from struggling backgrounds. When I first became aware I had been abused, I was asked to leave the small group Bible study because I was negative and pulling the group down. **What?** Kicked out of my small group at a church? I shortly left the church hurt and rejected at a time when I needed the family of God more than ever in my life. Thankfully my faith was strong enough that I knew God was faithful and that he would walk with me.

4) I had shared with some of my closest friends the secret I had managed to hide after my first bad encounter. I had shredded all my journals after I thought things were solved, but as you will see in chapter 9, I had strong remnants to deal with and obviously had stuffed too much in my impatience to heal quickly. I was triggered specifically by a male who was being dishonest.

He didn't hurt me, but I was shocked at how he could be so dishonest in the position he was in. I again quit sleeping, the panic attacks worsened, and I needed medication on hand for bad attacks as I would shake, sweat, become nauseous, and be unable to cope! I started journaling again and had taken my journal to work, and saw through a set of windows by fluke a friend reading my journal at my desk. **What?** Snooping through my private life without permission! I lost trust instantly in that friendship. I was having trust issues and more panic attacks.

5) After years of stifling my brokenhearted child within, whether consciously or unconsciously at times, she had now appeared again more stirred and seemingly even more desperate for help. I went to several sessions with a counselor (a Christian I had known whose area of specialty was sexual abuse), and after some initial work through some test, she suggested I might be lying about my abuse because I didn't fit into a timeline of abuse in the study. My developmental maturity should have been halted at some point and that wasn't apparent, so I could be lying. **What?** Who makes up panic attacks, nightmares, and wakes at two o'clock in the morning for months in a row and tries to cover this up in secret out of shame? Heartbreak yet again. A victim is only further abused with this accusation. My trust was rattled, but you will read later in a poem how this quickly changed.

How can others function so well? How many others do I see in a regular day who share the great loneliness of heart and shame of abuse? I needed a different type of book to help me on my journey. I pray this book about Molly and me can be that book for you.

These five situations have caused a continual stirring. The passion to write this book has only escalated over time. It has been an exhausting job as I have had to descend to my deepest heart and experience emotion related to deep scars that have healed but are not forgotten. I recently read a book about retirement and my heart, and head echoed this phrase:

Not writing a book can be more difficult than writing one.[1] (Zelinski)

So, here I go, forging a new path to write about a long journey taken. There is some risk to me, but I feel there is a higher risk in not helping others. I want to assist those on their path to healing from shame, loneliness, and despair. To know you are not alone in the journey will indeed help you. The journey can be both long and discouraging, but you owe it to yourself to be patient and seek the healing your heart needs. You have worth—I have worth. I do know that is almost impossible to believe that as your heart tunnels down to lonely and hurt places, but you have been created as perfect as a child of God, and He holds your heart in these difficult times when you are unable to. He will see you through in His perfect time, and He will continue to use your gifts and abilities to heal the hearts of others in time as well. You are not alone.

There is so much talk of post-traumatic stress disorder (PTSD) with the military returning from Afghanistan and other war-torn areas. PTSD is not limited to the trauma of the war zone, but also the trauma faced by victims of abuse. Victims of various traumas are on different journeys, but the road signs and paths to wholeness are very similar. Regarding PTSD, I wish at this time to acknowledge the movement to change the word disorder to either syndrome or injury as the word 'disorder' is not reflective of the external emotional damage done to the individual that has left these residual symptoms. However, as PTSD is most commonly used and recognized at the point of publishing it will be used in the document.

Take care of your heart and reveal it only very carefully. Learn from others to help your heart and mind. Take comfort in knowing it is a long journey, so be patient with yourself. You may have had your sense of worth stolen through abuse, but you are the vital link to restore that broken heart within you to wholeness. I say it now and again later: you will be your best counselor for your healing, and God is with you. Yes, the scar may remain but with work the pain will decrease.

> *Have patience with all things, but, first of all with yourself.*[2] (Saint Francis de Sales)

Physical Health vs. Mental Health

Physical health is a popular discussion item. You will often hear from others "Pray for me as I am going for tests and am nervous." When people announce physical illness, the casseroles start arriving for the freezer from people you may not have seen for quite a while. Cards, flowers, and visits accompany these freezer meals as well. Physical illness brings sympathy and the comfort of friends. This is true also with the loss of a friend or family member. Friends and even those who are almost strangers rally around to help.

Not so with the various aspects of mental illness, although there is a slow shift even in the corporate world. The feelings of loss and physical suffering with mental health issues are similar: you are alone as you are embarrassed to share. I understand that fear to share.

When you have been abused, part of you dies and a large injury is left to your heart. There is a sense of shame talking with others. There is a hole in your heart, but often no one can see it and many could not associate with that pain. We feel as though no one understands or cares. The heart and the soul slide further into chaos. There are more antidepressants prescribed than ever before, there are fewer people in churches, and liquor sales are up. There is stigma with mental health issues. Why? When will this change?

I remind you to take up the call to care for your heart. You can be the primary caregiver for yourself. That's right—invest in yourself and accept yourself as a one of a kind creation. God is walking with you and will help as He has helped Molly and me.

The Psalms

Each chapter of this journey begins with a quote from the book of Psalms. Many know Psalm 23 as the shepherd psalm and Psalm 121 as the funeral psalm, but there is a realm of topics in the collection of 150. While David, and several other writers, have not linked the specific trauma of sexual abuse to the writings, their Hebrew poetry resonates in the hearts of all who have suffered. Interestingly, one of my reviewers noted twenty-three chapters in this book and commented that it provides a similar comfort to one's heart as does the twenty-third psalm.

I am facing a transition from a sufferer of abuse who has journeyed to healing in a private situation to a more public author of a book with a difficult subject. For years, I have been inspired by the following quote and I relate that to the current transition:

I must be willing to give up what I am in order to become what I will be.[3] (Alfred Einstein)

I wrote that simple quote on two green index cards: one was in my study and one in the bedroom as a reminder to think of the future. At no time, do I feel this is a more accurate reflection of what I am doing than with the writing of this book.

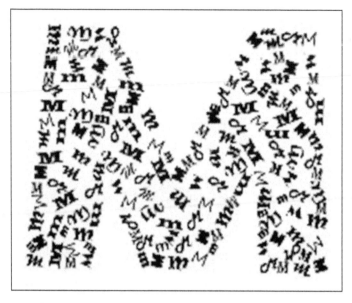

The symbol above is a large *M* filled with the many shapes of *M*s possible.

It is a reminder that the healing of the journey is complicated and yet beautiful.

<u>*Prayer*</u>

Gracious God, I write this book as a tool to help others. Bless the pages of this book and those who read them. May they bring peace amid stress and companionship in loneliness. To those who read to help themselves, give them comfort. May they see your love for them. Amen.

Book Layout Information:

1) Scripture quotes are in italics and are from NIV unless otherwise noted
2) Original prayers are bold script at the end of each chapter
3) Quotes from Molly's journals or poem books are in shaded text boxes
4) I specifically choose end notes as I want to give authors credit they deserve but didn't want to interrupt the flow of text for the reader
5) Tips at the end of each chapter include a project for the caregivers

PHASE ONE

The Discovery of Molly

Chapter 1

Molly's Mayday
What Is Wrong with Me?

Psalm 31:9–12

"Be merciful to me, O Lord, for I am in distress;
my eyes grow weak with sorrow,
my soul and body ache with grief.
My life is consumed by anguish
and my years with groaning;
my strength fails because of affliction,
and my bones grow weak.
Because of all my enemies,
I am the utter contempt of my neighbors;
I am a dread to my friends—those who
see me on the street flee from me.
I am forgotten by them as though I were dead;
I have become like broken pottery."

David and the Psalms

Not all Psalms are listed as being written by David, but this one is. Do we know what his specific struggle was that inspired Psalm 31? No, but he had several that we know of.

The Psalm that is usually associated with a heart of repentance is Psalm 51. Its background, which we look at later in the book, is found in 2 Samuel 11. David was lusting after Bathsheba, the wife of Uriah the Hittite. David asked messengers to go and get her. Then he slept with her, and she became pregnant. Then he plotted to have Uriah return from war to sleep with Bathsheba. Uriah didn't, even after David got him drunk. When David heard of this, he sent a letter to his army boss (Joab), requesting that he be put in the front lines so that he would be killed. The letter was sent with Uriah. Yes, that is correct. David sent a letter with the man whose wife he slept with and whom he wanted killed. Uriah was obviously a trustworthy man who didn't go home for sex with his wife and who didn't open the mail he was asked to deliver. Uriah was placed in the front row of battle and was killed in battle. David then took Bathsheba as his wife. Yikes. Adultery, then murder! An innocent man, Uriah, directly lost his life being a faithful servant because another man sinned. Not good. And even more difficult would be that others would know the truth:

- David sent messengers to bring Bathsheba;
- Bathsheba became pregnant, and all those around would know that Uriah had been away on the field with the army;
- Bathsheba then sent word to David she was pregnant through someone who would also know the story we expect;
- Joab, the army leader, must have known something was up for the request to have Uriah killed in battle when he was a soldier in their army!

So David clearly knew struggles of the heart as reflected through the background of Psalm 51. The emotion of this Psalm was due to his own mistakes that caused him anguish. We can identify with the trauma and shame of David's life experience.

Psalm 31

David could relate to a troubled heart. Different troubles, but troubles all the same. We all have different struggles, we have different support networks (or a lack of them), and our experiences affect our recovery from pain and distress. Can the psalmist empathize with your situation? Yes. David's feeling (31:12) was that of broken pottery. Most abuse victims are indeed that—feeling brokenness from pain and suffering from actions done to them. They have been dropped like a pottery dish and broken but not of their own error.

Distress and depression affect the heart, and can resemble broken pottery. The body is also pained and exhausted in sorrow, and anguish can overwhelm the mind. The great news is that as David bares his heart and soul to God, he receives relief and renewed hope by the end of the Psalm:

> *Psalm 31:14*
> *"But I trust in you, O Lord,*
> *I say, "You are my God."*
>
> *Psalm 31:23–24*
> *"Love the Lord, all his saints!*
> *The Lord preserves the faithful,*
> *but the proud he pays back in full.*
> *Be strong and take heart,*
> *all you who hope in the Lord."*

My hope is that as we journey together, you too can see your story through the eyes of another who has experienced a pain like yours. May you gain strength that you have not been deserted. God will restore your broken heart and bring a new depth of love. The journey from brokenness to wholeness is not easy. Many prefer the road of denial for survival, or suicide to escape. The road of escape is not one to which I feel we as believers are called to run. I can understand its lure.

Paul, in his writing to the Philippians encourages us all to *"continue to work out your salvation with fear and trembling, for it is God who works in you to will and to act according to his good purpose"* (Phil 2:12b–13).

This working out of one's journey and salvation is to be done even when it may be difficult! In completing the journey, there will be richness of reward and renewal of heart. Be strong and take heart!

Question: Am I willing to try the long journey to healing?

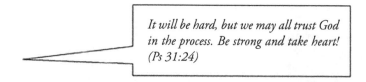

It will be hard, but we may all trust God in the process. Be strong and take heart! (Ps 31:24)

Meeting Molly

Molly is the name I gave my inner child many years ago. She looks similar to me in my youth but not totally: She has long red hair in two side braids with crazy bows on the end. She has more freckles than I could ever imagine on any child, and her eyes are always watching. She checks her surroundings, always knows where there is an escape route and has found places to hide in any new situation. She is wearing her favorite denim overalls with great big pockets to store anything she might need to feel safe, like candy or keys. I am sure if she were a child of the current generation, she would have her smart phone in there with her always!

A pictorial rendering of Molly drawn by a member of the Molly Project support team.

I knew of my inner child much sooner than my understanding of sexual abuse. Emotionally I was a stable child, but due to serious illness and near death at age three, I had a fear of hospitals and doctors. This seemed reasonable given the circumstances as it was a very stressful situation at an early age for my family and myself. I had been forecast not to amount to anything of value and to probably not live into adulthood. My parents were told I most likely wouldn't graduate from high school. This rocks the world around you, hampers your early success, and I am sure it changes how you are raised.

I was, thankfully, a fighter and so was Molly. Molly protected herself by hiding. The sight of any dental or medical clinic sent her shaking into what I identify as a little trunk in my heart. She seemed to be able to lock and unlock it from the inside. I never knew when she would overtake me with irrational fear, but my way to circumvent her unexpected arrival was to hide any illness and attempt to keep any signs of illness away from anyone best I could. I learned how to carry on as well as how to push myself through difficult things. I was going to beat the odds—I was going to fight my future forecast of impending doom. And I did. Doctors I had at that time would be more than surprised. I have coped with their anticipated brain dam-age well and lived long past the age of eighteen.

I knew something was wrong when I was triggered and had quit sleeping. Not just for a night or two. A loss of just a few night's sleep would be too easy to attract attention for me. No, my dear little Molly was rattling in her trunk. She was trying to let me know there were issues, but she was too scared to identify them for me. I went for months sleeping only until two o'clock in the morning. It didn't matter if I went to bed at ten that night, or one hour past midnight, or how tired I was, Molly and I only slept until two o'clock. Do you know how hard it becomes to function on a low average of sleep? I should say I worked a split shift job, which translates as a twelve-hour day in reality, so going to bed at an early hour was impossible when I was having supper at nine o'clock in the evening, had to settle the mind and walk the dog. I was also, during that time, in charge of a department at a university college and juggling responsibilities of staffing, budget, departmental growth, and a heavy teaching load. I made it through with no tarnishes, but it was an exhausting stretch. I am thankful to have been able to function, and I thank a few close friends for that.

It was a flashback that finally escaped from Molly's trunk. I could see everything—my view was from the corner of the small curtained stall at the hospital. Yes, there was early illness which was trauma enough, but here several years later I was to discover that in my almost teens I was sexually abused while in hospital. I had been, as I understand it, a fascinating research study project and spent a lot of time in our local children's ward getting tests after tests. They never seemed to ease the huge headaches associated with my illness, but I continued to be hospitalized. I hated my days at hospital—so much so I stifled the memories very well.

Now I understood. I lay on the bed, gown exposing all, my knees bent up, and there were doctors and interns "studying." Hmm . . . I was there for headaches and eye issues, there was no study subject below the neck! A repair job—for what? How did they explain this in their notes? I have wondered but never investigated. The shame I felt in that flashback. Many of you understand the pain, the shame, and the surprise.

I speak often of Molly and a trunk. This was a visual and not a suggestion one lock their inner kids in a trunk, or of course real kids either. It seemed to me that these strong emotions, which I later identified as a child I named Molly, hid out of fear. This fear was most likely that I would not accept this angry and hurt child. Maybe Molly's adult would not understand. Maybe the threat of identifying this pain was too much. This feeling hid for so long. Then the lid of the trunk began to slowly open. I expect one eye peeked out to see light first. Then maybe two eyes. Maybe the eyes found the light too bright and they found comfort in the darkness of the box. It might have been a hand that came out next to feel. This was the start of a new adventure. How would Molly's adult respond? This would take quite a bit of time as you shall see in this book.

Many children like enclosed spaces: tents, playhouses, forts, igloos, and closets. An area they could feel safe in and get away from the rest of the world for a bit. When Molly was in the trunk, was the lock on the outside for the adult to keep her there, or was it on the inside to keep Molly safe? This is a question I have asked myself frequently. I am reminded of the famous picture of Jesus standing at the door and knocking to be let in. What a beautiful image. Jesus could have walked through the door or he could have knocked it down, but he knocked peacefully.

Here I am! I stand at the door and knock. If anyone hears my voice and opens the door, I will come in and eat with that person, and they with me. (Revelation 3:20)

If you do an online search of photos of the scripture, it is interesting that many of the doors Jesus knocks on have no handle. Some do have exterior handles, but I do like the thought that Jesus left the opening to us. I take comfort in the thought that I never locked Molly away. I didn't even know, after all, that she existed! She locked herself in until she knew I was strong enough to care for her. I wasn't knocking on the lid of the trunk; she was well hidden. Poor Molly. I am so sorry for her now that I have understanding.

<u>*Chaos*</u>

The heart is stirred,
The pulse speeds,
The inner core shakes . . .

What is wrong?

Triggered?

Triggered by what?

Fight-or-flight reaction—fear has invaded.

It makes no sense.

The sensations increase,
I am going to be sick . . .
Yup . . .   . . .

> *... What is wrong?*
> *The inside doesn't feel right.*
> *Broken heart syndrome*
> *Why now?*
> *What happened?*
> *The unknown is somehow real.*
>
> *Feelings, skin crawling, heart pounding . . .*
> *The stomach feels sick, and I am getting hot.*
> *I feel dizzy, I can't think . . .*
> *My mind is a blur.*
>
> *This seems irrational.*
> *My mind likes to be in charge, but it isn't*
> *My mind has been taken over by my subconscious.*
> *I have dreams, I have photo images of the past,*
> *something has rattled my core.*
>
> *Oh goodness . . . how could it be?*
> *How could they?*
> *How could I have forgotten all this time?*

How did I not know? How could this memory arrive now in my thirties when I did not seem to know before? Why am I shaken to the core? How could no one have known at the hospital? Why wasn't I safe there? Why do I feel so terrible?

Could it be true? It was no work at all to discover that the lead pediatrician at the time of my abuse had died around the time my first flashback came forth from the deep recesses of Molly's trunk. He had, however, been charged with abuse, so my memory in the form of a vivid flashback could most certainly be real. Then I recalled my mother saying one day in passing that she never could understand why I would need a repair job "down there." Oh, it was a different time then, wasn't it? Some things were never talked about in regular English, but all around and hidden in a secret code. And then there was the letter she mailed me (while I lived at home as I recall) to say I should avoid taking the pill as it would have very poor effects on me. What? Where did this all come from? Why would she know this? I had forgotten those two comments from my mom until they made sense in my brain with the knowledge that I had been sexually abused in hospital during at least one of my long stays there in late elementary school.

(You may be tempted to ask, so let me tell you that I never told my mother of the recollections. I did not want to hurt her as she may have felt somehow responsible. She had taken me to the hospital many times, and she would have been horrified to learn of the crime they were committing. I know it wasn't her fault as this was a time when there were strict visiting hours and very poor communication. Mom has since passed, and it is time to free the last of Molly.)

What was wrong with me? I had intense feelings of shame and guilt that were not of my doing. There had been an invasion of boundaries and personal space, and there was sorrow, exhaustion, and anger. The emotions were hard to stuff! There was lots wrong. My little girl Molly had been attacked and for many years had hid this from me until she felt safe to open the trunk she had crawled into to hide, just enough to get some fresh air.

Back to Psalm 31

The Life Recovery Bible translates our portion of scripture as the following:

> *O Lord, have mercy on me in my anguish. My eyes are red from weeping; my health is broken from sorrow. I am pining away with grief; my years are shortened, drained away because of sadness. My sins have sapped my strength; I stoop with sorrow and with shame. (v. 31:9–10)* [4]

Sin does take a heavy toll on our hearts, as does shame. I see these two words as very different. I define the shame of the abused as the residue of sin done to us. We have not caused the sin; however, that feeds into intense feelings of shame. We are broken and our hearts ache, but **the sin of sexual abuse is not our fault** as we were not the perpetrator. The shame creates the feelings we read about in Psalm 31 that vary from distress, anguish, groaning, affliction, hopelessness, and terror to name a few. It is interesting to see this Psalmist makes a similar journey twice in the span of twenty-four verses:

Verses 1–6: struggle
Verses 7–8: praise
Verses 9–13: isolation and prayer in distress
Verses 14–24: praise

The journey in this Psalm is much like the journey in life; we often make a U-turn or take a detour for construction that can set our hearts back a bit on the journey. The most important is that we press forward to be more like Christ. Clouds and storms come, but the sun will shine again eventually. Do all you can to build your faith – imagine you are tending a small garden of sorts as it begins to grow.

Jesus, known as the light of the world, came to bring light, healing, and wholeness. Shame and stigma of sexual abuse and mental health issues may cause us to cover up because of feelings of rejection. In this cover-up there is darkness, yet we need the light to help heal. God is indeed our rock and fortress (Psalm 31:3), and He will protect us and heal us in divine time.

As we proceed on this journey, let me include a quote from Dr. Larry Crabb:

Christ wants us to face reality as it is, including all the fears, hurts, resentments, and self-protected motives we work hard to keep out of sight, and to emerge as changed people. Not pretenders. Not perfect. But more able to deeply love because we're more aware of His love.[5]

Work on matters of the heart is indeed work. We will be exhausted. Trust me it is worth it in the end. We will understand more of love and community in the process.

I was encouraged to hear a song by Christian artist Laura Story entitled "Blessings" when it comes to issues that create sleepless night. The chorus she sings refers to a possible three years of no sleep. She has walked through crisis and understands that God directs all.

> 'Cause what if your blessings come through raindrops
> What if Your healing comes through tears
> What if a thousand sleepless nights are what it takes to know You're near
> What if trials of this life are Your mercies in disguise.[6]

The text she chose[7] for the basis of the song was her life and the book of James:

> Consider it pure joy, my brothers, whenever you face trials of many kinds because you know that the testing of your faith develops perseverance. Perseverance must finish its work so that you may be mature and complete, not lacking anything. (James 1:2–4)

Like a switch

Rape as first sexual encounter . . .
How this changes one's life.
The pain, the sorrow, the loss.

Yet a switch was turned on
there was conflict
there was sorrow
Yet does it create craving?

A craving for positive relationship
for positive touch
for real care, not for selfish pleasure.
I yearn, yet at the same time I fear.
I need to be safe,
I need to be cautious,
I need to not feel . . .
It may cause reminder
I may not be as strong as I think.

Life is a balance, but for me
there lies curiosity:
is it possible to have pleasure?
The switch was turned on, but due to fear,
due to insecurity.
Action is dormant.

Dormant, yet
fear, jealousy, desire, loneliness
Such emotion for the victim.
Long-term emotional pain
for the selfish short pleasure of the perpetrator.
Unfair.
Painful.
A permanent wound and scar.

In Canada, we have a Bell Let's Talk Day. The corporation features stories of mental health and donates a portion of all communication towards healing of mental health. On January 27, 2016, Howie Mandel said (paraphrased slightly),

We go to a dentist for dental health, and no one blinks. We need to remove the stigma for mental health if we go to see a psychiatrist.[8]

Why do we feel those with mental illness are somehow not as good? Why are we embarrassed to cry in public? Why do we push people through mental health issues and feel sorry for them for physical health ailments? The tide towards acceptance of mental health initiatives is changing, but it will be a slow process, much like recovery from traumatic events.

The trauma from sexual and physical abuse as well as other types of PTSD, and the chemical imbalances part of our genetic codes all work together to create instability that our conscious minds are unable to control. Through these unfortunate assaults on body, mind, and spirit, we become shaken. We lose our confidence and our sense of wholeness. We become detached from ourselves and from others at a time when we need others the most for our healing.

Prayer

Creator God, help. I am overcome by chaos in my heart, and it is flooding over into my mind. I did not know why I reacted to certain things, but now that I do, I am filled with feelings of anger, frustration, and confusion. I feel terrible, and I need your help. Amen.

Chapter End Projects

Shame is a common feeling for victims of childhood sexual abuse. It is an inner feeling of filth and stress. It can make one feel nauseous, cause panic attacks, and bring depression and a total lack of self-worth. It is a clear sign of abuse even if one doesn't recall the specifics yet.

1) Ponder times when you feel overwhelmed with grief and sorrow. Ask yourself if there is a trigger or something that may have caused these feelings? Try making a list of what these are. Try to describe the feelings in words. This can be a helpful but very difficult step.

2) Take some time to recognize you have been broken. Your personal space was invaded. Know this is not because of any fault of your doing as a child. Know the age of consent in your province and country, ponder voting ages and when you can get a driver's license or be allowed to drink. Those give you a timeline for when you can make decisions for yourself and protect yourself. If you were attacked prior to that age, you need to know you have no guilt in this. Find some old pictures of yourself at the age you were assaulted and see how innocent and beautiful you were as a child. This will remind you the abuse should not have happened to you. Write about how this makes you feel. Take some time to yell at God about how you feel. He understands, and it is good to communicate honestly. If you were an adult at the time of attack, you may be more likely to recall the incident but even more likely to feel that somehow you allowed this to happen. Your no meant no even if the abuser did not hear it.

3) **Analyze your situation now and ask yourself if you need urgent help.** You may need to go to a medical doctor for advice and help and you may be recommended on to a counselor. **Go. Get the help. You are worth it.** If you have

a close friend or family member you can trust, go and talk to them. Or even just tell them you are depressed even if you can't say why. If they do not respond with care, shake the dust off your feet as they say, and go find another friend to help. Remember you are worth it!

 Tips for Caregivers

1) This is a good time for you to do some self-reflection. And if you can come to a point where you feel for past hurts and mistakes, this can be helpful for you to help someone else. I don't suggest you tell your story to journey with the one to whom you have been called to mentor as that may only be a detraction. Your first goal is to ask about their story and access whether they are in urgent need of professional intervention or not. That is key. Make sure they have the healthy support system they need to journey safely.

2) Do some research. Find some books that might be helpful for your friend to read but make sure you have read them first and feel they are appropriate to the situation.

3) Offer to go with the hurting to see a pastor or a counselor for help. Doing this on one's own is stressful. Even if all you do is drive them and wait in the waiting room, you are serving as an important part of the healing team.

Chapter 2

Molly's Mire
When Will You Heal My Heart?

> Psalm 102:4
> *"My heart is blighted and withered like grass."*
>
> Psalm 34:17–18
> *"The righteous cry out, and the Lord hears them;*
> *he delivers them from all their troubles.*
> *The Lord is close to the broken-hearted*
> *and saves those who are crushed in spirit"*

A withered heart, a blighted heart, a broken heart. These images are clearly experienced by those who have felt the brokenness of sexual abuse. For many, the subconscious has hidden the trauma and has worked hard to patch the heart and press on. But the patches wear down, revealing the heart still in shreds and in need of a real repair. Duct tape has been an amazing invention of the twentieth century, but it does have a best-before date too.

The Lord is close to the brokenhearted. We may not always feel that or understand that, but His ways are not our ways. His ways are better, and we will grow to understand that. He will indeed save those who are crushed; we need patience, and God can grant that too.

Question to ponder: How can God renew the crushed spirit or a broken heart?

God will "save those who are crushed in spirit" but how, and more importantly, when? With the realization of cruel action against me in my childhood, my heart and confidence sank. I began a period of grieving for Molly, in a sense taking over some of the grief she had locked in her safe hiding spot. I found myself wearing black all the time, and started antidepressants to cope. It seemed there were no pills to allow for sleep as Molly was stressed. We would feel the need to run, not sure whom I thought I was running from, but it didn't seem to matter. I would get in the car, lock Molly and myself in, and head for a highway. I would turn on some tunes and drive until my spirit was more settled then I would turn around and drive home. Somehow the open road gave me a peculiar sense of freedom and control. I started escaping in the car Sunday afternoons and exploring different roads and places. Sometimes I experienced anger, sometimes sorrow, but more than anything it was confusion.

How could I not have known? I felt I was not as smart as I may have previously thought. Feelings of insecurity seemed to take over my mind; self-worth was devastated in this discovery of hurt and pain. I looked around at people thinking they all seemed to be doing so well, and I was completely distraught. I became impatient with myself; it seemed I could neither remember nor forget. My current mind seemed to have been hijacked by feelings and emotions of the past, and I was unable to control these thoughts. As months went on, and I became exhausted to the core, my number one petition with God was, "when?" When would God get around to saving me from a side of myself that was overwhelmed with heavy sorrow? When would I be whole, and when would Molly pull herself together and leave me alone?

It was many years later, and many chapters to come, when I realized I shouldn't hate Molly for interfering with my current life. She needed the care that I could show to others but not her. In my first few years, I admit I hated this side of me that was dark. There was shame, a feeling that overwhelmed, that even now is hard to put my finger on. I wished I could find the off switch for my screaming inner child. I was trying to find a way to hide her back in the trunk she was trying to escape from. All she wanted was love and care, but she was interrupting my life.

I felt I did what I could. I started slipping into a neighboring city to buy books on sexual abuse. I didn't want to be seen by anyone in that section of a bookstore or library and be recognized in the city I lived . . . or have a student of mine ring these through the till. How embarrassing that would be! Abuse is about secrets, and I didn't want to be public at all. I was going to use my brain to read, research, and be healed! Ha! I had a lot to learn about recovering from trauma.

After much reading, I piled the books in the corner (well hidden). I thought that journaling might help. I wrote and wrote . . . anger, discouragement, fear, other memories. During this time, there seemed to be a great divide between my real life of work and my home life of struggling with what at that time I might have called the Molly issue. I felt my spirit dig deeper into what seemed to be a black hole. Molly cried and screamed, and she had what I would say was irrational fear. I, the adult, was rational, thinking, and mature, and she was . . . well, she was losing it! She wasn't healthy for the rest of my functioning, so I needed to find a quicker fix.

My physician had been aware of my need for antidepressants, then sleeping pills, and soon realized I needed more help. She called the provincial medical association to discover there was help for patients abused by medical personnel. A first appointment was arranged, and the counseling was free. I needed only to drive nearly three hours one way for each one-hour appointment. On the first drive, I was so nervous that the joy I had once experienced in my car was now lost. I was taking this crazy inner child Molly to a counselor to be fixed. I was stressed. I had needed to take time off from work (an entire day). What if people found out?

This is silly, I thought to myself in the session. I can't even talk about the issues. Here I sit with a young female therapist hired by the medical association to help those in my situation, and I feel too weak, too insecure to function. **I am a teacher at heart and very seldom lost for words, but the entire English vocabulary was gone and seemingly not at my disposal.** I sat like a stiff robot pinned to the chair. I was finally able to talk about work a bit . . . but all I seemed able to do was have myself speak of the adult and current issues. I couldn't elicit any text from Molly, and we both shared an overwhelming feeling of fear and chaos. What? I would need to book another appointment? Are you sure? No magic wand? Or maybe the release of leaving this office would provide all the healing I would need?

I can't recall how many sessions I attended, but I must have driven that poor therapist to insanity each hour! She knew why I was there, but I surely couldn't talk. Molly and I didn't feel safe, and this was all a waste of time. I needed a day off work each time, which wasn't easy to do running a university department. I was busy and too important for these days of silence and I was getting nowhere. I stopped going.

Okay, back to the question of "when, Lord?" I read every book I could find or order online, I had filled several journals with complaints and frustrations, and counseling with a specialist had taken me nowhere. The book of Job in the Old Testament speaks of God allowing tests against a man he loved. Yet the turn from devastation and sorrow can all be read in a short afternoon. Of course, it was much longer in real time for Job, but I made the comparison in frustration anyhow! How could my issues continue to drag on through months and months?

I have always loved watching murder mysteries on TV. I loved the series *Murder She Wrote*, which first aired on CBS in 1984 and has done many reruns and now has a set of books. There was always a murder, and sleuth Jessica Fletcher could always get the crime discovered, solved, and return to her pleasant Cabot Cove home for a cup of tea in the span of sixty minutes, and with time for commercials as well. Surely this crime committed on Molly so many years ago could be soon wrapped up? I would plead with God that surely one more hour would be sufficient.

The hours added up. They became weeks and months. I would be exhausted and nearly falling asleep in the day, but night time would arrive and I would watch the hour hand slowly spin by. I would get up and have hot milk, try reading, watch some news on TV, then crawl back in bed and watch the hours spin until the alarm went off. How long one can go without sleep before death, I wondered, but I merrily tackled each day trying to stuff Molly away to cope with the required routines of working full time. Considering all, it went very well. Unbelievable.

> *It takes tremendous energy to keep functioning while carrying the memory of terror and the shame of utter weakness and vulnerability.*[9]
> (Bessel van der Kolk)

How many other people lay in their beds awake, I wondered? Never in my life had sleep been difficult, but now the ordinary task of resting one's head on the pillow to enjoy eight hours of sleep was no longer possible. Sleep had become a luxury I was not able to afford.

Molly had taken me on a whirlwind journey of sorts, and neither of us was sure when the maze[10] would stop . . .

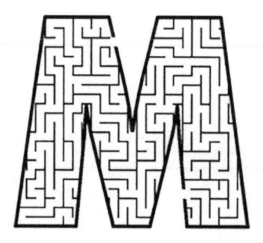

The sludge of heartache would not dissipate. Was there another book I needed to find that would have a magic solution for Molly? If only there was a business for mental disaster services that could find their way in to either head or heart with some type of vacuum system to remove the mud left by Molly. It was a heavy black sludge that weighed down my heart for sure, but was also challenging mind and body to their limits. Why couldn't my cognitive side overtake the situation? Why was I not able to reason with Molly? Surely, she has another side other than just feelings of humiliation and irrational fear. She shakes in her trunk, and my core rattles. She is neither present nor absent but rather an odd mix and usually at the most inconvenient times.

My mind grew impatient. How can the mind be so inferior to the subconscious? How did Molly become bigger than anything else in my life?

<u>What happens to me when I get triggered and have a panic attack</u>?

- My hearts pounds within.
- My eyes feel like they might bulge out.

- I often feel like my skin is crawling. Hard to explain but maybe you can relate.
- I can feel sick to my stomach and ready to barf (and often have).
- Diarrhea within minutes.
- Sometimes I feel dizzy.
- I often overheat instantly.
- I feel a fight-or-flight response. I must look like a deer in the headlights.
- I'm often aroused just by a sense of panic.
- Heavy heart, I feel a pressure in my chest.
- I suffer inability to sleep.
- I'm unable to slow the brain down and can almost feel it working!
- I just feel odd.
- I feel loss of confidence, which escapes like air out of a punctured balloon.

Thankfully as I read this list, I realize have not experienced these for quite a while, which has been confirmation that I am either finished or nearly finished my journey! Yippee! However, for those of you experiencing these reactions to trauma, I am sorry. I know it is hard to function and feel like a sane participant in the human race. I empathize with your struggle.

It is amazing how many psychological problems involve difficulties with sleep, appetite, touch, digestion, and arousal. Any effective treatment for trauma has to address these basic housekeeping functions of the body. (Bessel van der Kolk)[11]

It is hard to define what a broken or crushed heart can feel like under the weight of shame. You may be able to relate to some of these responses I have had. Or, you may wonder if your experience is real if you don't have a selection of these from my list. Remember, we are all different and this is not a competition or survey. Our trauma is different, we are different, and our journeys to healing will be similar but also different.

A damaged heart
Does a heart that has been broken truly heal?
How long a process is it?
With God's help, couldn't it be instant?
One touch,
One zap to recharge,
One spray of Creator's glue . . .

We are to be made whole,
We are washed to be whiter than snow,
But do the scars ever heal?
Are they always a memory?

Is a heart made new better than the original?
Healing seems to be such a long process . . .
A little at a time,
What I can handle only. . .

A thorough cleaning job is intense. There is
  dust
  mold
  rot
  peeling
  stain
  injury
  memory
  agony
  fear
  confusion
  chaos
If one's heart is not the same, will it be accepted?
Will a new heart receive the transfusions it needs to survive?

Oh Lord, repair my broken heart . . .
That I may be healed and speak of Your Power and Love.
Provide for me the courage to
  face the truth of my past,
  the strength to survive the present,
  and a renewed hope for the future. ...

> ... Hold me tight in Your arms of love until I can again walk free as Your chosen child.
> Stir in me Your Spirit
> > that I may have the confidence I need
> > to complete this work in you.
> Amen.

Psalm 34

The righteous cry out, and the Lord hears them;
he delivers them from all their troubles.
The Lord is close to the broken-hearted
and saves those who are crushed in spirit (Psalm 34:17–18)

A broken heart and a crushed spirit. The Hebrew word for broken used here is shabar, which means "to burst." So, whether the heart withers in sorrow or explodes with troubles, or breaks under the weight of our cries, we read that God will indeed save us.

Definition[12]

Original Word: רָבַשׁ
Transliteration: shabar
Phonetic Spelling: (shaw-bar')
Short Definition: break down, break down, off, in pieces, up, brokenhearted, bring to the birth, crush, destroy,
    A primitive root; to burst (literally or figuratively) -- break (down, off, in pieces, up), broken((-hearted)), bring to the birth, crush, destroy, hurt, quench...

This Hebrew word study suggests a positive aspect of a broken heart that brings hope—that through the pain of a breakdown there is potential for new life and growth. This is best visualized for me with pine and spruce cones that explode during a fire and create new a new forest through that heat and destruction. In other situations, seeds may have been dormant for some time due to weather, dry conditions, or because they are too deep in the soil to see sun. All seeds contain potential for new life and are not forgotten. We too are not forgotten. While repair may not be possible with the figurative old heart, God can transplant anew with new birth arising from the breakdown. He does save those who are crushed in spirit, and there are so many reasons we have crushed spirits. There are also many symptoms from a broken heart, and many of them are explored in upcoming chapters of this book.

I want to turn our thoughts to the responses that sexual abuse cause that many are not conscious of. From what I have seen and read, I suggest that most abuse victims are changed one of three general ways as a response to the trauma they have faced. Victims can be turned on with a strong sex drive, be turned off with no sex drive, or be numb. There are many stages within these three as you can imagine, but this is an important discussion regarding response and recovery from abuse. Those abused will usually slot better into one of these even if they are not aware of the damage done to them until much later in life. I have arbitrarily chosen letters for each. See figure 2:1.

Figure 2:1 Extreme response levels to sexual abuse

Victim A (turned on)	Victim O (shut down)	Victim B (turned off)
Multiple Partners	No response to intimacy	Abstinence
Works as a prostitute	Lack of emotions	Fear of intimacy
Boundary issues	High boundary walls	Lack of interest in those the same gender as abuser
More likely to abuse others	No threat to abuse others	No joy in sexual relations as it may cause too much pain emotionally

Where might you place yourself in these categories? You might also be tempted to judge one category as better or as worse than another, but all three have been similarly damaged. Figure 2.1 is based on my own pondering after reading many stories of survivors. I further take that understanding and attempt to remove and notion to look down on one response over another. This approach I feel makes it possible for us to provides God's healing to all who encounter sexual violence without temptation to first judge them.

Figure 2.2: Why Victims A, O, and B are similar?

---

1) All three have been wrongfully violated.
2) Most have struggled with depression at some point in their adult lives.
3) It is very possible that many were not aware of their abuse when they seemed to slide into the personality of Victim A, O, or B.
4) All these victims, no matter what their life response to the abuse, need love and compassion as their hearts ache.
5) At a deep level, all three types struggle with loneliness and restlessness.
6) They have extreme levels of shame in their lives.
7) All victims of trauma or those suffering from PTSD are responding radically to their abuse even if subconsciously.
8) All victims need to be able to love themselves and accept the past—this can be VERY hard.
9) With effort and direction, Victims A, O and B alike can learn to achieve a healthy balance in their lives and care for others.
10) They can develop healthy relationships.
11) They all will benefit from higher understanding of their situations and the effect on their lives as this will allow them to be patient through the healing process.

How is it that one person can be spared from the Victim A outcome of abuse or another person spared from the flashbacks of memories? That I cannot answer, but all I can say is that all our situations are so incredibly different. In fact, as you read this book, I wouldn't want you to compare your journey with mine as they won't and shouldn't match. We will have many of the same issues of shame and feelings of worthlessness, but our journeys will be different.

Back to my ponderings on the three responses a victim can have. I can give you the reflection from my own experience: I have been on the Victim B extreme. I have been afraid of intimacy because of my own feelings of inadequacy and shame. I subconsciously felt stressed around guys but didn't know why. I have not married but I see that marriage would have been a strong trigger for me and more than I could have handled before I went through this whole process. It also didn't help that I did not have a positive role model as for a father . . . that too had me very consciously wary of men. That may have been a gift to save me from relationships that could have been heartbreaking until I was able to be aware and heal from the abuse I suffered.

As a Victim B, I have felt alone in many regards but there are many like me. I have just finished reading a book by Beverly Engel. She has been working and writing about sexual abuse for thirty years. She herself is single and knows that was due to her abuse issues. She quotes in relation to her disclosure that "**childhood abuse, and the shame that comes with it, affects our ability to connect with others in an intimate way.**"[13] You may know this from your experience, and I empathize with you. I have many connections and friends but not what I hoped and longed for. While so many friends are married and have the thrill of seeing their genetics flourish through children and grandchildren, I have not had that chance. At weddings and family events, I feel sad and lonely. I am sure this is related to my past abuse. I know this loss is due to the abuse having resulted in a heart that is slow to trust. This I have discovered in hindsight only. Even after understanding why I was cautious and now feeling healed from the abuse, I still mourn being single. Family times of Christmas and Easter are still tough. Those from large families do not know the questions of "where are you celebrating Christmas this year" can be painful.

For those of you who struggle with being alone in your grief as I felt in my past, please read this prayer aloud and know God hears you.

Prayer

Lord, my heart is broken. I am filled with shame. I am lonely. I am restless. I am unhappy. I hate myself. I feel lost. I am tired. I long for help. My heart aches. Help . . .

Chapter End Projects

1) Take some time to grieve. We are often taught to hold our emotions in, and we are too embarrassed to cry. **Don't be ashamed of feeling shame!** Do not stuff these feelings any longer. Find a place to sit, bring some tissues, and just feel. It can be hard for sure. The opposite of not feeling is death, so experience these feelings no matter how hard they are as they are part of the life process. We will all have sorrow, we will at times all be sick, and we should express these feelings at each of these times. Many cultures publicly grieve for the death of a loved one; I wonder if they have it right by allowing themselves a time of mourning where they wail and wear black. This can be helpful. Usually there is a time limit for mourning, which is also good.

So, are you ready? It could be time to cry for you. Your inner child has had much sorrow and loss. She/he has hidden this for a long time. These emotions are built up more than you can ever imagine. Let them out. You have suffered a huge loss, and you have carried this on your own for too long. If you don't feel sorrow or anger for the crime committed against you, maybe you have difficulty releasing emotions. I might suggest you get a movie to watch that may help you. That movie choice can range from cute Disney story to biography or love story. The themes can be of your choice, but the goal is to tap your emotions that may have been stuffed for quite some time.

2) Make a list of responses you have when triggered.
3) Think of something you would like to do for you and your inner child. Maybe getting an ice-cream cone of a crazy kid's flavor or a bag of cotton candy. Or maybe you want to go on the Ferris wheel at the fair. Or maybe watch a cartoon Saturday morning while you are in your PJs. Make a list of a few fun things to do for you and then do one this week! Plan ahead. Make a special event for you. We

can and should plan for some fun as well as pondering and grieving.

 Tips for caregivers

1) Try your best to put yourself in the shoes of the one you are helping. Listen to their stories, feel the pain of being alone and feeling shame with them. Your ability to feel will help them and you will grow at the same time.

2) Make sure you remind the individual you are helping that they are valuable and that it is important to search for these feelings. Accept them and love them as much as you can. This is crucial in the healing process. You are serving as the hands and feet of the healing God who is very much a part of the process.

3) As you seek to serve and give as a fellow servant of God, make sure you invest in yourself as well. You need some light and some humor to balance out the heartache. You too may stay awake at night feeling sorrow and anguish.

4) Pray for God's direction and strength. Wait before the master healer for guidance. And get help yourself if the weight is too heavy to carry. Try not to reject the already rejected abuse victim but tell someone in your circle that you are assisting in an important intervention so they know how to care for you. This will not be a one-hour visit but a long-term commitment.

Chapter 3

Molly's Muddle
Why, Lord?

> Psalm 35:22–23
> *"O Lord, you have seen this; be not silent.*
> *Do not be far from me, O Lord.*
> *Awake, and rise to my defense!*
> *Contend for me, my God and Lord."*

Wake up, God. Where are you? Isn't that something we have all said? Especially when we see destruction, hardship, and of course abuse? We wonder why God takes the life of a vibrant pastor at an early age in the peak of his/her career and yet the dishonest CEO continues to live a selfish and comfortable life. As a famous book by Philip Yancey is titled, *Where Is God When It Hurts?*[14]

Does God rise to the defense of those He loves, or is this just a myth from biblical narrative? I will repeat throughout the book that God's ways are beyond our understanding. We see with very limited vision because we are human and not master creator, the great shepherd, or powerful king. The psalmist cries out for God to contend for him, to argue his defense or to support his vision. One needs to ask if the psalmist got himself into this trouble himself by unwise choices. On the other side of the thought process is of course for the one who lives as close to 100 percent close to the heart of God, why does God allow this? Why is there pain and suffering? We have experienced pain and suffering since the fall of Adam and Eve in Genesis 3. God spoke that he would increase pain of childbirth—is this a sign of a loving creator or one who sees punishment as the response to disobedience? God is also judge not just friend and shepherd. Yet . . .

One question always stands out to me, and I expect it is true of both mental and physical pain: How could a loving God allow painful hardship to those He loves, to those He created? While my head does understand that rain falls on the just and the unjust, my heart struggles at times. Yet I place my faith and hope in God. He cares about the sparrow, so I know He also cares for me. This is a song I have loved since I first heard it:

"His Eye Is On the Sparrow"[15]
Poem by Civilla Martin, Music by Charles Gabriel, 1905

1. Why should I feel discouraged, why should the shadows come,
Why should my heart be lonely, and long for heav'n and home,
When Jesus is my portion? My constant Friend is He:
His eye is on the sparrow, and I know He watches me;
His eye is on the sparrow, and I know He watches me.

Refrain:
I sing because I'm happy, I sing because I'm free,
For His eye is on the sparrow, and I know He watches me.

2. "Let not your heart be troubled," His tender word I hear,
And resting on His goodness, I lose my doubts and fears;
Though by the path He leadeth, but one step I may see;
His eye is on the sparrow, and I know He watches me;
His eye is on the sparrow, and I know He watches me.

3. Whenever I am tempted, whenever clouds arise,
When songs give place to sighing, when hope within me dies,
I draw the closer to Him, from care He sets me free;
His eye is on the sparrow, and I know He watches me;
His eye is on the sparrow, and I know He watches me.

Question: How could God have allowed this to happen to my heart?

> <u>Where is the easy button?</u>
> How can I remember all and get through?
> I see images, not full film . . . why?
> Am I not able to handle it all?
> Will all the memories ever come?
> Do I need to fear the future?
> Do I truly need to see all and work
> through all to be healed?
>
> Is there an off switch to give my mind a rest?
> Is there an easy button to speed through the path?
> Is there a way out?
> Will I make it?
> When?
> . . . ?

How many times over the last many years have I asked my friends when will I feel better? MANY times! They were patient with me and continued to say they had no idea when the journey will be done. The good news is that if I am still breathing, then I am indeed growing in my relationship with God and in the process of recovery. The key word there is *process*. It is not an easy journey, and there doesn't seem to be a quick escape route. One can of course slide into denial and say there is no reason for such pain, or become a workaholic so there is not time to hear the inner child scream. Conversely, one can take the time to experience the emotions, care for oneself, and stay in the process to a point of recovery. And of course, if I am still living and breathing, it means the journey is not done, but the difficult climbing could be.

Why? How? When? Who? Where? What? So many questions and most of which I am unable to answer for myself let alone you. The "when" question is just one of a list of questions that are too hard to face.

Thoughts from Psalm 35

This psalm written by David begins with a petition for God to fight against those who fight against him. We read, "Arise and come to my aid," this sounds very much like a contemporary 911 call. This reminder for God to get up is resounded again in verses 22 and 23, which I have chosen as the highlight theme of this Psalm. The contemporary language could be something like this: "*I have had enough! You have seen what is going on God. Get up and do something. Now!*" We all have felt like that at times and for many different reasons as we are not very patient. We live in a world where we desire instant. We used to wait weeks for mail across continents, but now when we wait two seconds for an e-mail to send we begin to get impatient!

Another theme we read in this Psalm is "how long" (verse 17), which is the constant cry of most who suffer any type of illness. We want all healing to happen quickly, and many of us seek vengeance as this Psalmist did too. Frequently David reminds God to bring a spear or have his enemies fall in a pit. These thoughts are best in one's private prayers!

One important phrase from this Psalm that should encourage us all is that God does see all (verse 22). For reasons we can never fully know, God allows sin to happen. God has seen, God knows, and you may feel as though he is not acting. His timing is different than ours. One cannot assume this shows a lack of care for us. God cares deeply for us. Each of us. As he cares for each sparrow, he also cares for each person he has created. He wants to be in relationship with us.

For many people, it is through the valleys in life that they come to God or experience a new depth with Him. In fact, many artists whether musicians or visual artists report their best moments of creativity come during hardships. As you heal from the abuse you have suffered, may you rest next to Jesus. You are not alone. God is with you.

So, those questions of "why did this happen" and "when will I feel less crushed" will continue. Possibly for quite some time. I have no concrete answers for your journey. Sorry. It is for you to walk, but you are not walking on your own although it may feel that way. Next to you walks God who created you and loves you as you are. You may wish to repeat the phrase uttered by David of "awake and rise to my defense." Be contented with the idea that our God who watches the sparrow and allows rain to fall everywhere is watching and does care deeply for us. It will take time. I was comforted reading the following in a book by Ellen Bass and Laura Davis:

Moving on is tricky business for survivors. It cannot be rushed. It cannot be pressured from the outside.[16]

We want to ask many questions, but do not push any buttons to rush the process as it will intensify with neglect. Be content to ask without forcing an answer. Time is needed to solve many things. Be open to all the feelings you have and accept them. Remember all you can remember. Hold your heart close to you, give yourself a hug. Take care of little things that you can and leave the other things to God for now.

Life is like riding a bicycle. To keep your balance, you must keep moving.[17] (Albert Einstein)

You will search for healing and continue to question why until you have recovered as much as can be. Then you will be able to look back and see with better eyes. Then you will understand better the grace of God in all things. For now, however, be content in the muddle.

I received my first muddler as a gift a few years ago, and I didn't know what it was. I learned it is designed specifically to smash up fruits, herbs, and spices to create amazing cocktails. I am not much of a cocktail drinker and not a maker at all, so this bartender tool sits patiently in its original plastic wrap in my secondary utensil drawer. A tool designed to mash and increase flavor? I ask myself if our hearts being in a muddle is a good thing. In hindsight, writing this after the healing process is complete, the muddle can be a good thing. It is easy to just slide through life without thinking. We go to work, come home, do our routines, watch news, and go to bed until we start over. Our best work can be done when we stop to think and when we go through hard times.

I have been a lover of the music of Ludwig van Beethoven since I can remember. I was amazed at how his best works came **after** he began losing hearing and after there was no external sound at all for him. All his musical sound became internalized and in a sense more muddled with the emotions of what he was going through as an artist.

> *Oh, Providence, grant me but one day of unclouded happiness, for true happiness has long since ceased to echo in my heart. Oh when, when, Divine One, am I to feel it again in the temple of nature and of men? Never? No, it cannot be! Oh, that would be too cruel!* (Beethoven)[18]

During this writing of what became known as the Heiligenstadt Testament in 1802, Beethoven was also writing his Symphony No.2. There were many symphonies and other compositions to follow as Beethoven lived until 1827! This time away to ponder and write about the sorrows of not being able to hear ultimately led to a new musical style of writing that gave us lyrical melodies, rich harmonies, and intensity.

As we who have been abused muddle through our individual journeys, we may wonder and question as we feel crushed. There is no easy button, and often a lack of answers, but know that God has seen everything and our gracious God will work for our problems. I am reminded of a poem I wrote while in the Alberta Rockies, and I share that with you now.

Growing up

Growing up . . . past the first stage of life:
past the desire to be first, past the desire to
be great, past the desire to keep up.

The journey is about me. It is not being jealous of others
or struggling to be someone I was not created to be.

The journey is about giving up—letting go.
In doing so finding myself and a
deeper relationship with God.

Yes, there is a giving up of sorts.
A death to new life.
Much like the death of Christ and His resurrection.
This is a giving up of me:
the handcuffs . . . the shackles that I have left on myself.
I need to give them over.

The image came in prayer, prayer that
somehow, I could forgive and be free.

The caterpillar is loathed by many for munching on
trees. They are killed (bullied) because they are deemed
as bringing a death of sorts. Yet if they survive the
first life cycle, they wrap themselves up; they cocoon.
That may be seen like a giving up of sorts, but it is
necessary to allow for a second more beautiful stage.

The caterpillar pulls away from the world,
hibernates, ponders, and is reborn into
something more beautiful.
It has to wriggle out of the cocoon in the perfect time.
It can't rush; it can't be impatient.
It must await God's perfect plan.
There is no other way.

Then one day that former fuzzy and hated
crawly thing wiggles and wiggles.
It is wet and soggy in its new form.
It seeks to dry off in the sun . . . dries
one wing, then the other . . .   . . .

... Then it must try something new: forget
about crawling and start to fly.
Here the once hated creature is now
appreciated for its beauty.
It flies majestically, seemingly unaware
of previous struggles.
It is free.

Lord, I need to be free that I might serve you . . .
that I might draw closer to you.
I thank you for the image of the butterfly.
I thank you for real butterflies.
I thank you that you care for me as
you care for every sparrow,
every seedling, every soul.
I praise you today as I try to wait
patiently in my cocoon . . .
Waiting for Your call and Your touch.
Thank you.

Prayer

Lord, where are you? How could you have let this happen? How long will my shame strangle my heart? When will I feel normal again? Will I feel normal again? Help me . . . help me trust you, help me accept my thoughts, help me to accept my feelings of intense shame . . . help me wait. Amen.

Chapter End Projects

1) Use this picture[19] as a starting point. (If you don't have another, try drawing a sparrow.) When doing so, notice all the detail within this simple bird. If you have a chance, go out and watch some sparrows for an afternoon and ponder God's creation.

2) Make a list of questions you would like to ask God directly if He were to show up at your door one afternoon for coffee. Ask the tough questions like:

- Why did you let this happen?
- Do you really love me?
- When will I recover?

Make the list and have it ready. You don't need to look for answers yet. Keep getting those questions written down.

When you have the list ready (and this may take you a few days), then try the following prayer outline:

God, this is _____. I come to you today because my heart is crushed. It has been hurt by someone else, and I need help. I also have a list of questions which I read to you now.

. . .

. . .

. . .

. . .

. . .

Thanks for hearing my struggles. Help me sort them out. Thank you. Amen.

 Tips for caregivers

1) Remind yourself and those you minister to that all is in God's timing. Oh how we wish to have control in the details, but we need to trust. Ponder ways to assist others to develop patience to wait and allow them to feel more contented while they wait.

2) Consider a gift to help them when they are discouraged: a candle to light when they are lonely when you aren't there, or maybe a plant to admire, or a rock to carry in one's pocket?

3) And of course, continue to pray for healing. God is faithful and does love all created, but often it takes time to experience this love after a deep injury to the heart.

Chapter 4

Miserable Molly
Why Do I feel So Alone?

> Psalm 10:1
> *"Why, O Lord, do you stand far off?*
> *Why do you hide yourself in times of trouble?"*
>
> Psalm 4:1
> *"Answer me when I call to you,*
> *O my righteous God.*
> *Give me relief from my distress;*
> *be merciful to me and hear my prayer."*

In the eyes of the writer, God seems to be missing in action. God has no need to justify His actions to the psalmist. The faith and experience of David bring him to realize God is bigger than all else he can know. Is God further away, or is our need to be close to our loving God who will keep our hearts safe even more important in these times of trial?

Deep pain and sorrow changes a person. No question! Whether the change is ultimately positive or negative, we are changed through the journey. The journey of abuse causes the heart to ache. Nothing seems important anymore. Why go to the movies, why save money for the future, why bother trying to care for others when the pain in your own life is so overwhelming? Joy in the little things is shaded over by anguish. We are somehow backed into a dark corner to ponder and mourn.

The cure for this darkness must surely be antidepressants, right? I went on them for a time. I felt at first it was an excuse or failure on my part, but the energy drain on one's body and mind to deal with conflict can only wear down one's chemical balance. I am sure the medications helped my mind, and while it didn't cure my life, I am sure it helped my stamina.

I encourage you to seek the help of a physician if you haven't already. Prescribed medications under the watchful eye of a physician can be helpful. The percentage of people on antidepressants is apparently quite high. Trusting medical science in the development of pharmaceuticals is one small step towards healing. It is not a sign of weakness but a willingness to be as mentally strong as one can be for the journey. Much like the athlete with the science of Gatorade, the abuse victim will be feeding her mind with the tools to assist the process. Alcohol and street drugs are not the answer; they are used to cover up and camouflage the pain only. **To deal with the pain (feel it, understand it, and take baby steps to recovery) takes the highest level of courage and endurance.** Those who seek help should not be looked down upon in society. Somehow it is okay to be sick of body, but those who are sick of heart/mind/soul are placed lower in the minds of others. Is this pride on their part? Or do they just have no idea of the pain one may face if they are abused? They should be thankful and desire to help those whose hearts ache with sorrow and loneliness.

From Molly's Journal
November 16, 2011
A Deep Well

Sometimes I feel too deep for others. I've had lots of pain and hurts, and my heart does go down very deep. The water is probably nicer at a deep level. Purer and maybe more "original." However, it is considerably more work to get there. And, I see how often I could feel lonely because many relationships never have the time to go this deep. Two reasons: 1) It is a lot of work for people to get down that deep to find me, and 2) it is often a huge climb for me to come out and meet people above the surface."

I have never felt so alone as when made aware that I had been abused. I, however, was not near as lonely as poor Molly must have felt for years being tucked away with her memories and trying to keep them all inside.

If you were abused as a child, you are likely to have a childlike part living inside you that is frozen in time. (van der Kolk)[20]

I like the phrase "frozen in time" in the above quote. Being cold also reminds me of being alone. The heart is cold until love and care touch it. Reaching that cold inner child is a lot of work but will be worth it in the end.

<u>Why do I feel so alone?</u>

Lonely . . .

People everywhere
I look into their eyes to look for life.
Are they just playing a game?
Are they superficial?
Have they truly entered their inner world?

I have a deep well—
made deep through pain
made real through honesty.
This means true friends must be deep as well.
I am lonely with acquaintances.
I need depth.
I need love.
I need tenderness.

My heart is deep also because it is being kept safe.
It is scared to connect.
At its depth, it is very vulnerable.   . . .

> ... This heart has dug deep looking for
> living water—for refreshment.
> Yet the deeper I go it seems the lonelier I become.
>
> Alone, but praying God continues to be my guide.
> With Him I have hope.

Psalm 10:1 WHY?

The psalmist, who without knowing if God is near, worships God but still questions. It is not wrong to question. That is how we best learn and grow. Why are you so far off, the writer asks? Why do the weak and wicked seem to win? Verse 15 of Psalm 10 begs that God break the arm of the wicked and evil man. Many read these imprecatory psalms as too negative and recommend they be taken out of God's Holy Scriptures. Yet God is not afraid to be questioned. He does listen to His children. He is very patient with us when we see the small picture only and not the overall view. The psalmist feels God isn't doing anything, but we see that is not the case as we continue to read through to the New Testament and finally the book of Revelation.

Please understand that I too would prefer that only good happen to people and that there would not be evil in the world. I too feel that it seems unjust that some have suffered in life and others do not. God has said in scripture that it does rain on the just and unjust alike (Matthew 5:45), but I can relate to the psalmist. Why did I have to get sick as a child? What potential did I lose in life? Why was I abused during the research years to follow? What did they learn that cost so high a sacrifice for me? Why does God seem so far away?

I ask the same questions as above on your behalf: why did God allow this to happen? I am sorry to say I have no specific answers, but as I have travelled in my journey, the pain has lessened and I see the bigger picture. May this provide hope for you. I too, like the psalmist, shook my fist at God, developed a hatred for all doctors and for all who are dishonest. I have been envious of those that seem to have it all, which in my mind is an athletic physique, a well-paying job, a nice house, a good marriage, and family.

Psalm 10 ends with the following shift in emotion with what seems to be no transition from hatred to acceptance:

> *The Lord is the King for ever and ever; the nations will perish from his land. You hear, O lord, the desire of the afflicted; you encourage them, and you listen to their cry, defending the fatherless and the oppressed, in order that man, who is of the earth, may terrify no more.* (Psalm 10:17–18)

May the end of loneliness come soon. While we have just read that the psalmist has turned from mourning into acceptance, this is not the final time we read of anger or hear questions. So it is with us. There are times we move ahead a step but then feel we move backward. In time, as the healing progresses, the good days will outweigh the negative. The psalmist repeats his questions, and so will we. The psalms represent real struggle, and real life. This back and forth of emotion reminds me of Jesus on the cross. He knew His life mission was to die for our sins and be resurrected to provide new life for all, yet despite that He was also human and struggling with the same emotions as us. Listen to these words spoken:

My God, my God, why have you forsaken me? (Matthew 27:46)

Yet, while also on the same cross around the same time, he also says, "**Father, forgive them, for they do not know what they are doing**" (Luke 23:34).

Jesus was both fully man and fully God, which we can see most obviously in the contrasting emotions of loneliness and care for others we read about in the gospel accounts of the crucifixion. There are other examples of emotion reflected in the life of Jesus. Remember the story of Jesus at the temple? Jesus had been predicting his death and training His disciples about forgiveness, patience, God's work, and more. Then we read of His triumphant entrance into Jerusalem (the story of our Palm Sunday reenactments) and the crowds spread their cloaks and chant, "Hosanna to the Son of David" (Matthew 21:9).

Within two verses of Jesus being announced as prophet, he goes to the temple. One would think he would be there to pray to His Father in heaven, or to do some very religious ceremony. Well, Jesus does do something. Most of us watching would say He had a temper tantrum: He drove out the merchants selling items intended for worship (doves for example) and overturned all the tables. Were any animals killed by his violence? It doesn't say, and while I wouldn't want to read that into Scripture, we must ask ourselves what was damaged when Jesus was done. He was making a point that some should not profit from worship and that what was needed was prayer, but for the actions of the future king, this behavior was unacceptable. Jesus was feeling intense emotion no doubt due to the sorrow he felt upon arriving at the temple. After this outburst of rage, we read that the blind and the lame came to Jesus for healing and they were healed. They were not afraid of this man from Galilee who had just overturned tables and could overturn them as well in their weaker state. They came, and we read they were healed.

The healing process will present a variety of emotions. We need to be sad and grieve for our own losses. It is okay to be angry at injustice done. It is not unusual to feel intense shame as mentioned previously. It is best for us to feel these emotions. Stifling them, either consciously or unconsciously, only delays their healing.

So, ask and ask and ask! Argue with God as He can take it. We were created with emotions, and we need not be ashamed of how we are feeling. What we do with those intense emotions, however, will be our responsibility. Heading out to murder our rapist because of intense emotion only makes matters worse for ourselves. Covering up with alcohol and drugs is also not a good response as that affects our ability to function in the present and can interfere with our work and home lives.

Trauma, whether the result of something done to you or something you yourself have done, almost always makes it difficult to engage in intimate relationships. After you have experienced something so unspeakable, how do you learn to trust yourself or anyone else again? Or, conversely, how can you surrender to an intimate relationship after you have been brutally violated? (Bessel van der Kolk)[21]

<u>Alone</u>

Years alone . . .
Wondering what everyone else was doing
while I lay in solitude.
Today I had a horrible onset of a cold.
I have been in what I would call an alert coma
Alone, sad . . . reminded of the past.
The loneliness, the darkness.
Ears alert to what might be happening
in the world around.
Am I safe?
When will someone care?
When will I be better?
Where is God in this pain?
God is Healer . . . what is it I must learn?

My hearts needs healing,
it needs care.
it needs to be first, not last.

Who can understand?
Who would really want to care?
Am I actually loveable?
Not sure . . .

I will try to hold on tight to God's hand and
trust Him through all of this.
He has been good to me
He will be with me until the end.

How does one filter these intense emotions spoken about in this chapter? Some things I have tried which seem to be successful are to journal and to find some friends who I can trust. You may need the help of a counselor. I have read of others in this journey of healing that have often taken up to five years of regular counseling with a therapist. That can seem expensive for sure, but worth the investment to keep you safe and on a journey to renewed health.

The goal of our many questions may not be to expect obvious answers. But facing the questions and the emotions behind them opens the door to healing even if only by a slight millimeter. Any amount of light into a totally dark space will make a change for the better!

As long as you keep secrets and suppress information, you are fundamentally at war with yourself. Hiding your core feelings takes an enormous amount of energy, it saps your motivation to pursue worthwhile goals and it leaves you feeling bored and shut down.[22] (van der Kolk)

Pray with me:

God, I am lonely and my heart is broken. I am sad and feel intense shame. Guide me through these painful memories and help me to see you. Lord, walk with me, carry me, hold my hand, and hug me when my heart is weak that I can carry on serving you and live my life to its highest potential. Thank you. Amen

Chapter End Projects

1) Take some time to think about when you feel most alone. Is it when you are with people? This is quite common as it is often in large groups where you see others relate and connect? Or is it when you are at home by yourself? Or maybe it is at church? You may look around the congregation and feel no one else seems to have any issues and you don't fit. This is of course not the case, but we all become experts at covering up struggle as it seems to reveal weakness. Write down some specific memories you have where you felt so alone your heart felt crushed.

2) Next, spend some time thinking about where you are most happy and feel most connected with yourself, with others, with nature. Make a list of those times and places that you recall. They could also be times with someone who is a great encourager to you. Think of one thing you could do now to help offset the sorrow in your heart and do it: go for a walk, have a bath, watch a candle burn, go to a concert, go to your favorite restaurant, find a friend who loves watching movies with you.

3) Over the next stretch of time, and with your two lists of moments where you feel alone and moments when you feel connected, try to find a balance. Imagine you have placed these in an old scale. I have that image for you here, but you need to mentally place the items to achieve balance. The world likes to steal from the positive side, so you need to make some investments there.

 Tips for caregivers

1) Send a card. Maybe the old-fashioned way rather than a quick online card via e-mail. This card will be something to display and to reread over and over.

2) Another suggestion would be to offer to go with them for an event that might otherwise be difficult.

3) You may also best be able to judge whether the one whom you are caring for may need the help of a physician to rebalance from the drain of stress. You could make a recommendation or go with the person as they seek help. These are difficult steps for many. Going to a doctor for cold symptoms is much easier than for stress.

Chapter 5

Molly's Mistrust
How Can I Trust?

> Psalm 12:1–2
> *"Help, Lord, for the godly are no more;*
> *the faithful have vanished from among men.*
> *Everyone lies to his neighbour;*
> *their flattering lips speak with deception"*

Honesty . . . integrity . . . sincerity . . . these three words are most difficult for an abuse victim. They may have trusted their abuser. In my case, it was a medical professional who was expected to take care of his patients and put their best interests first, not his own lust and selfish desire. For others, it can be a parent, an extended family member, a brother, a teacher, a pastor, a boss, etc. These would all have been people once respected and in many cases idolized. Yet how could they lie and cover up such a grave crime? They are dishonest with themselves and dishonest with others. They have stolen the innocence usually of someone entrusted into their care, and they usually deny the incidents if confronted. They know they have committed an atrocity, don't they? Yet they go on to commit another by not being honest and therefore accusing the victim of deceit when they have endured enough pain already. How do they do this? Answers like, "She led me on," "She agreed," "He didn't say no, "Her dress was too short," "She is making that up," "It was consensual," and on and on.

We all do it—we all have some level of dishonesty. There are the little white lies to protect someone or create a surprise, which is intended for a greater good and seen as okay. Once we move past the white lies, there is every color and shade known in full color spectrum. Why? We usually lie to make ourselves look better. Maybe we have success with those around us, but the lies are known to God and us. How do we manage to pile up the lies so easily and quickly?

Coaches, celebrities, pastors . . . profession, lifestyle, or public status does not limit the abuse of others. Just as we walk at night in a large city with our guard slightly up, we need to be cautious of situations around us. If one's home has been broken in to, one of the first things they do following the crime is install a security system. Too bad that wasn't done before, but we learn from our experiences. If someone has come in and violated your home space by hunting through drawers, taking precious items and irreplaceable heirlooms, you have a new fear, a level of insecurity.

It is the very same for ourselves. If our body has been broken in to, we put our guards up and experience a heightened sense of fear. Fear is an opposite to trust. When someone has hurt you deeply, you may never regain that trust again, for good reason. Relationships change from situations encountered, and some relationships cease. Often these feelings are transferred to others as they may also do the same things. That is fear. That is loss of trust. That is not a surprise.

> *Abused children "learn to always be on alert.*
> *To be ready for danger."*[23]

Many survivors are on hyperalert; this has been how they have protected themselves from further abuse. We have fears that many others do not have. These fears keep us awake at night, affect our eating, affect our interactions with others, and are very difficult to resolve.

> *For our physiology to calm down, heal and grow, we*
> *need a visceral feeling of safety. No doctor can write a*
> *prescription for friendship and love: these are complex*
> *and hard-earned capacities.*[24] (van der Kolk)

> *Trust*
> *How can one regain trust?*
>
> .
>
> .
>
> .
>
> *One must know truth*
> *One must see compassion*
> *One must feel love*

Psalm 12

Back to the Psalm for this chapter and the thoughts that the faithful have vanished. It may indeed seem that way. It appears at times there is an absence of God around us. We as children of God put our trust in others to be honest and genuine. It is difficult to be both godly and regain trust in those who are not. The phrase "flattering lips" suggests boasting and a sense of pride. In flattering someone else there is usually something to gain. We have several expressions for that in contemporary English like "brown nose" or "suck up," and they are quite negative. They reflect deception and create a sense of lost trust.

The psalmist begins with a sense that we are no longer godly or faithful. What are we doing? And where indeed are the faithful? Where are we putting our time and energy? We need the faithful serving and ministering in the world to provide healing for those who desperately need it. We all have a mission to fulfill the commission Jesus gave us to go into the world and help (Matthew 28:16–20).

The psalmist sees trouble and negativity. These things are indeed easier to see in the midst of struggle. In fact, in darkness it is difficult to see anything. The hope one has in this Psalm is that even though humankind is sinful, arrogant, and dishonest, by verse 6 the psalmist reminds us that the words of God are flawless. Hence, we see the two extremes in the psalm: people who we are wary to trust and God who speaks the truth. Thankfully, the second image can carry us through when we have trust issues!

This chapter is entitled "Molly's Mistrust." What trust issues did I have? Well, first off, the medical profession for sure. Even though I didn't recall the incident for years, I knew I had a hatred of all things medical, but I assumed that was related to my sickness as a child. The second trust issue that I was aware of was sharing my pain with people. I shared the experience in the introduction about the small Bible study at the church I was attending and was told I was too down to be in the study and asked me not to come. Are you kidding? What that translated to was a fear of sharing how I was doing and knowing I would struggle with acceptance. I did tell a few at work because I was needing time off; the stress was high, and I was sure it was obvious. As for the church, it wasn't long until I left there. I quit going to church for years even though I had a good relationship with God through my entire process. Quit going to church, you say? Yes, because like the psalmist said, the godly and the faithful didn't seem to be at a church I could find in the community I was at; and I was, at the time, too emotionally weak to search very much.

This fear of being rejected at church is a present reality as well. I met with the pastors at my current church early in 2016 to let them know I was leaving my full-time job to write a book and let them know what it was about and shared my story. I asked if it was okay I stay at the church. Other options could have been using a pseudonym for the writing of the book or else being prepared to leave. They were sure my story would be accepted, so I press on in my steps of trust. Now as you notice during the edit stage it was recommended I use initials rather than a full name. Once this book is published I do hope to connect and minister by retreats and public speaking, but the layer of anonymity provides both safety for me as well as enhancing the desire that this book not be about me but about God's work in our lives and God's love for you.

The mandate of the church should be to help those with struggles. But maybe we are too worried about looking right or behaving right? What would Jesus have done? In His ministry here on earth, Jesus healed the woman who had been unclean for years. He did the "disgraceful" thing of speaking to a non-Jewish woman. He "worked" on the Sabbath to help others. He showed patience in the garden when the disciples fell asleep rather than staying awake with Him in His last hours. He showed patience with Thomas when he needed to see the hands and side of the resurrected Christ.

What might Jesus have done with me if this situation was time travelled back into his ministry on earth? I doubt Jesus would have kicked me out of church or rejected me because my heart was broken. He reached out to people even when this meant breaking the Jewish rules and traditions that he was born into and knew. Jesus was most present in New Testament readings during people's crisis. He didn't turn them away even when crowds were following after Him. Jesus would not have been content with the shame I felt with church and church people. He too would have echoed the text of the psalmist that the faithful seem to have disappeared.

It is far too early to discuss regaining trust in situations for you as that is a very slow process and needs the reading of the entire book as a starter. But I can say that God has been faithful to me. The healing process has been slow, but as in real life, the deeper the cut, the longer to heal.

What about you? You may feel rejected by those around you, people whom you would have wanted as part of your support system. They may be too overwhelmed. They may have stuffed a similar situation in their own hearts and can't help you. Although it may be difficult, shake the dust off your feet and move on. God will take care of you in His timing and master plan. Continue your journey even though you have lost trust for the time being in humankind. It is these same humans that will be essential in the healing process.

Let's ponder the church again. Are we ungodly? Do we hide behind the clothes, the cheery disposition, and are we afraid to share how we really feel? Do we, in church, truly care for the neighbor in the pew or chair next to us? Are we just covered up? Do we act like Christians Sunday mornings a bit like the chameleon or gecko lizards that can camouflage themselves into any color in a matter of seconds to better match their background environment?

If we are indeed called by Christ to serve, we must be honest, we must be ourselves, and we must communicate things of the heart. If we build walls around ourselves or try to make ourselves look better by flattering speech, we are unfaithful.

As for you and your broken heart, take care of it. Protect it. Share it with those you feel will protect it with you and learn to forgive those for whom this task is too hard as they have their own journey to travel.

Prayer

Lord, help me to trust, first with you and then myself. Then, as I gain strength, help me to trust a small circle of others for healing. Also, help me to weed people out of my life who stress me and are in the way of my healing and safety. Teach me what it is to trust again. Give me the strength to deal with issues of my heart. Amen.

Chapter End Projects

1) Who has shaken my trust? Who do I feel is hurtful and selfish? Are they like this to others? What turns me off at this time? This could also be helpful to share with others around you, maybe a family member, maybe a fiancé? If others care for us, they will benefit from knowing our road-blocks and fears as that will assist them to help us.

2) Who do I trust? Make a list:

3) Why do I trust them? What have they done or not done that I feel safe with them?

4) What do I need to see in others to feel as though I can trust them? Honesty? Appreciation? Generosity? Solving this can help you in your personal growth as well. It may also help you in relationships now and in the future.

5) What do I feel I need in a friend right now? A new friend may take a while to come, but this is crucial. It may be a paid counselor, it may be a pastor, or it might be an instructor you trust. It doesn't need to be a permanent choice. Remember, our lives are in flux and we all change in time.

 Tips for caregivers

1) The most important tip is to be as faithful as much as you can. The broken heart will strengthen when it is cared for. Imagine yourself as a netting to hold delicate sweet peas as they begin to flower and grow to the sky. Of course, you can't be there at all times but send a quick text. Stay connected as you are able, as you could be the main healing balm God has chosen to help.

2) Ask if there is something you can do to encourage or build trust. It is difficult to read minds. Trust me!

Chapter 6

Mellow Molly
Why Is My Spirit Quiet?

> Psalm 30:1–3
> *"I will exalt you, O Lord, for you lifted me out of the depths*
> *and did not let my enemies gloat over me.*
> *O Lord my God, I called to you for help and you healed me.*
> *O Lord, you brought me up from the grave;*
> *and you spared me from going down into the pit."*

Healing comes in stages. That was and still is an important lesson for me to know, so I pass that along. You will have times where all seems smooth. You think you may have passed through a phase and maybe dealt with all healing already. As you will learn from my experience in chapter 9, it doesn't mean you are finished the journey, but stopping to take stock and give praise for little things is very important. Imagine it as coming up for air after a deep dive in a swimming pool: some needed fresh air and freedom. It is good for your physical body as the adrenaline you can use up with emotional work is quite amazing. Adrenaline is a hormone that kicks in at crisis moments and allows us the energy to get through. Like a line of credit, constant withdrawals can create stress on the adrenal glands and they need time to recover. So a rest and some quiet time isn't a bad thing for sure! The Bible refers to this rest as a Sabbath—something we are more inclined to forget about.

Please read the following about the Jewish treatment of the Sabbath day as recounted by the BBC:

> *Every week religious Jews observe the Sabbath, the*
> *Jewish holy day, and keep its laws and customs. The*

Sabbath begins at nightfall on Friday and lasts until nightfall on Saturday. In practical terms the Sabbath starts a few minutes before sunset on Friday and runs until an hour after sunset on Saturday, so it lasts about 25 hours. God commanded the Jewish People to observe the Sabbath and keep it holy as the fourth of the Ten Commandments. The idea of a day of rest comes from the Bible story of the Creation: God rested from creating the universe on the seventh day of that first week, so Jews rest from work on the Sabbath. Jews often call the day Shabbat, which is Hebrew for Sabbath, and which comes from the Hebrew word for rest . . . The Sabbath is part of the deal between God and the Jewish People, so celebrating it is a reminder of the Covenant and an occasion to rejoice in God's kept promises . . . Shabbat is a time with no television, no rushing to the demands of the telephone or a busy work schedule. People don't think about work or other stressful things. In order to avoid work and to ensure that the Sabbath is special, all chores like shopping, cleaning, and cooking for the Sabbath must be finished before sunset on Friday.[25]

In reflection, I am not very good at Sabbath. No TV? No phones? No rushing or cooking? How many of us can go twenty-four hours (or twenty-five for the Jewish Sabbath) without their cell phone and not feel as though they have lost a piece of themselves. However, this idea of Sabbath is modelled after God taking a day off after the creative work. For six days, the creator worked and then followed with rest and reflection. Resting one day a week to focus on the creator is important in our lives.

It is good to put all aside to thank God for our many blessings and take time to rest with family and friends. The Christian Church refers to Sunday as our Sabbath, but we have not kept the day free. We go out for lunch (making others work on a Sabbath day), we head to the mall, or we can often be seen doing laundry to get ready for the next day at work or cleaning. Malls used to be closed because no one would ever consider shopping on Sunday. Now we want all twenty-four-hour everything may it be groceries, banks, medical clinics, etc. I am guilty of this too.

Investing in solitude time when going through healing, whether physical or emotional, is very important. You need some time to mellow your Molly equivalent. The author of a book I read recently on abuse talks about imagining the child within in a rocking chair on your lap. Invest time to hold on to your aching, crying child. Hold her until she becomes quiet as she too will need some rest!

Please let me hold you. I want to be the grown up you never had, the one who really listens to the things you have words for and don't have words for. I want you to be exactly who you are. You don't have to be a convenient, considerate, cheerful child the way you were for (mother). I rocked and held myself until the sobs diminished.[26] (Jane Rowan to her "little Jane")

What a caring image of sitting with your inner child to help her heal. In many ways, we will spend most of the time doing the work of healing by ourselves. There is no cure but patience and time.

Psalm 30:1–3

Looking at the Psalm for this chapter, many of us can relate to the cry to be lifted up! "Lifted me out of the depths" in some translations appears as "drawn me up" with the visual of being in a deep pit and being drawn up in the equivalent of a water bucket. Depths reflects a deep well—deep sadness and struggle that David's enemies could well have gloated over. The reference to calling to God and being healed is found in a new translation by Pamela Greenburg as

God, my Physician, I cried to you for help, and you healed me.[27]

(Pamela has a master's in Jewish studies and her book is a refreshing translation of the Hebrew poems.)

This psalm is very personal in nature. In the NIV translation, I/me/my are used eight times in the opening three verses. The text then turns towards a call for worship of a larger group ("you saints of his") because of God's healing of the psalmist. God's actions to the psalmist are threefold in the opening verses:

1) Lifted out of the depths– could be sadness and depression
2) Healed me– could have been a physical or mental affliction
3) Brought me up from the grave– sounds more like a rescue from physical death for illness or injury

Three reasons to give thanks. Listed as three they give a stronger argument although it could have been just one rescue to spare the psalmist. The psalmist took the time to make a list. With Twitter, we have learned to shrink language to communicate, but in so doing we can lose both the meaning and emphasis. The psalmist could have said one word: *rescued.* But with the depth of language used, we can also see the depth of suffering incurred by the psalmist. Much was needed to be done to bring relief and, obviously, it was.

I am reminded of the many testimonies I have heard. People tell a story of their own lives to encourage others to thank God for work done and at times help to illustrate that the God we worship is one of action. He is not just a far-off being, but rather one who is interested in each one of us. Our stories, even if they aren't the very end of the journey, can provide hope to others.

As you have some mellow time, take stock of three things to be thankful for and why that could inspire someone else. We need to remember to give thanks for healing we receive at all parts of the journey. We may indeed move from one mountain to climb to another, but when we experience a plain with lovely meadow flowers, we need to stop and give God praise for accompanying us on the journey. Mellow can mean relaxed, subdued, peaceful, and content. Compared to the busy of stress and flashbacks, dreams and fears, it is a nice break. Try to enjoy moments of mellow and Sabbath in your life.

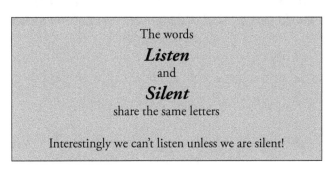

The words

Listen

and

Silent

share the same letters

Interestingly we can't listen unless we are silent!

Figure 6:1 Things Molly (and her adult) are thankful for

Item	Why
God's presence	I feel safe with God watching over me
God's faithfulness	He understands and is always there
God's healing	My mind and body feel relieved even if for only a short time
Friends	They have taken the time to listen and care which is a precious gift
Books	Authors who have written about their journey to give strength to others.
Counselors	For not looking at you like you have gone insane when you talk with them
Life	The chance to process, heal, and journey and for a future to shape
Her adult	For believing in her and trying to help
Childhood	As it is never too late to experience a happy childhood

Back to the idea of a Sabbath, I recently read a book that had a most interesting view of the term *Sabbath*:

> *Resting in the Lord doesn't mean doing nothing. When you rest in the Lord, you abandon your own frail attempts to live and allow the Lord to live through you. You cease from your own works just as God did after He created the universe.*
> (Kelvin West)[28]

Yes, resting is a good idea. And we can trust God to direct the journey!

Prayer

Gracious God, I thank you that you walk this journey with me and that you carry my heart when it is too heavy for me alone. I thank you that you have helped many others on their journeys and that gives me hope as I travel my journey. Thank you as well for this time of rest. Help me to breathe and relax. Give me rest for the remainder of the journey. Also, help me to see others along the way who need help. I may not be strong enough to do much more than say I understand, but that can be encouragement enough. Thank you for holding my heart tight when the going was tough. I will speak of your wonders when I am stronger. Amen.

Chapter End Projects

1) Reviewing a project suggested a few pages ago, what three things are you thankful for right now?

2) What do I like doing if I have time? Make a list of twenty-five items—yes twenty-five! Expand your horizons, reach out of the box you have been in, and imagine. It may be something you have never tried but would like to.

3) Another good way to take some time off would be to practice unplugging. Tell everyone you are taking a "vacation" and will be unavailable. Then feel free to take a "staycation" where you stay at home with your phone, Facebook, and computer off. Just time for you and your pets and family. Do not feel you need to follow up with work or anything else. Just take time for you and do what you want. Maybe it is sleep. Maybe not. It is okay to put yourself first while you journey from grief and loss to a point of healing. It is unfortunate that we can't enjoy time off with no responsibility more often, but a day or two here and there are good. Try to avoid tackling a work project like cleaning the garage or freezer. They may help you feel better superficially, but you can find another day for that. For myself, I have often run away to a hotel in the city I live. Someone will make the bed for me, and I am in a new spot without the clutter of usual life. It is relaxing and refreshing. Try a new hotel in your own city and you will be surprised!

4) Take some time to hear God. Be still and listen. Be thankful. Write a list of one hundred things you are thankful for. You started with a list of three above, so you have just ninety-seven to go. That is possible! It could be a taste of a perfectly ripe peach or the sunset colors at your favorite beach. A hundred can come quickly if you take the time to do it.

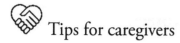 Tips for caregivers

1) This chapter has been about rest. As a caregiver, you need to make sure you are getting adequate rest to be the strength you need to be. What can you do for yourself today? What in your life have you put aside that would feel better getting completed? It is important you invest in yourself. It also helps to model a more balanced lifestyle to those around you.

2) How can you encourage those who are helping to rest? Can you take their kids for an afternoon? Can you invite them to your home or cabin? Can you find a hammock to loan them for their yard for the day? There are so many options here. Many of them do not require your time or expense but just some planning.

Chapter 7

Muted Molly
Where Did Molly Go?

> ### Psalm 37:1–7
> *Do not fret because of evil men*
> *Or be envious of those who do wrong;*
> *For like the grass they will soon wither,*
> *Like green plants they will soon die away.*
>
> *Trust in the Lord and do good;*
> *Dwell in the land and enjoy safe pasture.*
> *Delight yourself in the Lord*
> *And he will give you the desire of your heart.*
>
> *Commit your way to the Lord;*
> *Trust in him and he will do this:*
> *He will make your righteousness shine like the dawn,*
> *The justice of your cause like the noonday sun.*
>
> *Be still before the Lord and wait patiently for him;*
> *do not fret when men succeed in their ways,*
> *when they carry out their wicked schemes.*

Hmm. It has been quiet for a while now. All must be solved! Excellent. Let's reread those journals and then throw them out. I wouldn't want anyone to see them that's for sure.

Hmm. It is still quiet. My heart is less stirred, my heart rate is lower, and I am able to sleep. Thank God for that! You will too when you know that God is indeed in control. We do not have all the answers; in fact, many times I can feel I have few answers but many questions. Taking some time in quiet is good . . . right?

Psalm 37:1–7

This psalm is a classified as a wisdom psalm. It holds truths for humankind and sounds more like a teaching reminder. It doesn't contain worship to God, nor does it speak directly to God as many psalms do. It is also an acrostic poem in that each double verse starts with the next letter of the Hebrew alphabet. A repeated theme in Psalm 37 is "do not fret" (vs 1, 7, and 8), and the reason is explained by what God will do in the future: "They will soon wither . . . they will soon die away . . . He will give you the desire of your heart . . . He will make your righteousness shine." This is a reminder that God's work is done in His time not ours. We need to be mindful of God's timing and not our own needs and desires. This is a very difficult task.

We discussed a similar idea in the last chapter when we encouraged Sabbath time. Now the lesson is to "be still before the Lord." Okay it is one thing to relax and fellowship with friends and family on a day off, but it is quite another to be still before God. Waiting in a sense. Hmm, I don't do that so well either. I think to my last line up at a grocery till, or phone call to cash in air mile points when they interrupt to tell you how much longer you might have to wait. Turns out I may not be as patient as I should be. Resting in the Lord and being still before Him involves trust in His plan. We have the duty not to fret about our situations but to turn our attention to the truth that God is in control of all things even if we are unable to see that in the present. Oh, if we had foresight . . . Ponder back to hindsight moments in your life and how you have seen God in them, and it will be easier to trust in the future work of God as well.

Take some time right now and think about God's work in your life in the past. Think about when you have seen His work most obviously in your life and start making a list. Think of ten things, and then while you are busy waiting before God, think of ten times ten more things. Thank Him and then remember He also has your future planned better than you could ever do it! I encourage you to be still before the Lord and turn your eyes on to the works He has done. If you want to follow the lead of the psalmist, try writing an acrostic list of things to be thankful for. I have a blank chart for you in the projects section, but below I provide an acrostic of what I am thankful for. This is not as easy as you might think to complete!

<u>Molly and her adult's acrostic list of things they are thankful for:</u>

Letter	Thankful for:
A	Acceptance
B	Bible
C	Candles
D	Diversion
E	Empathy
F	Friends
G	God
H	Hugs
I	Intellect
J	Justice
K	Kleenex
L	Laughing
M	Melodies
N	Nature
O	Observation
P	Patience *(I guess)*
Q	Questions
R	Restoration
S	Sleep
T	Tears
U	Understanding
V	Voices
W	Writings

X	Xylophones
Y	Yokefellow
Z's	*(Okay, that is a stretch but if you have gone for long periods of time without sleep, two references is okay)*

If you wanted to follow even more closely the model of Psalm 37, an acrostic poem, it could look like this:

A little girl name Molly
Became very troubled
Cold and dark was her place
Damp with tears
Eventually she reached out
Forgetting her fear
Gasping for breath
Heaving with heaviness
Into the subconscious
etc.

When you have carried a heavy weight for so long, it is easy to let go, but can you believe it is possible to miss that weight too? We are creatures of habit and often struggle with change even if it is for the better.

When Molly became so quiet, I was worried I had scared her right off. Maybe she had once again locked herself in a trunk in my subconscious and needed to hide. Was it something I did? Or maybe something I didn't do? Should I worry? What should I do now?

Could it be that I had become used to the panic attacks, fears, nightmares, and triggers that I am more comfortable with them than without? Does calmness have me unsettled as it is a foreign experience?

I need to remember to be still and wait for God at all times, not just when it is convenient for me or when I feel like being still. I need to learn to wait at all times. Waiting involves a sense of trust. Like an engaged woman waited for her husband to return home from war, so my heart needs to wait on Molly to speak and God to heal. It is not always easy, but enjoy the glimmers of hope. The times when you feel rested even when you aren't sure why. God will be faithful.

Prayer

Lord, help me not to fret in good times or in bad. I need to learn to be still before you, but that takes a calmness and a trust, which does waver in my heart. Help me wait. Wait with me. Remind me to dwell with you because with you I have everything I will ever need. Thank you for the work done in my heart this far, and thank you for your patience as we together complete the journey. Amen.

Chapter End Projects

1) Take some time to pray. Make a list of ten things to be thankful for today and include them in a prayer to our gracious and loving God.

   10 Things to thank God for today:
   1.
   2.
   3.
   4.
   5.
   6.
   7.
   8.
   9.
   10.

2) We learned about acrostic poetry in the book of Psalms. Try an acrostic list as Molly did in the chapter earlier.

Letter	Thankful for:
A	
B	
C	
D	
E	
F	
G	
H	
I	
J	
K	
L	

M
N
O
P
Q
R
S
T
U
V
W
X
Y
Z

3) Plant something, preferably indoors where you can keep a close eye on it. I recommend you do it from seed. If you don't want to wait too long, I suggest a bean or a sunflower seed. The goal here is to have the opposite visual presented in our reading for today, which spoke about evil men withering like grass. We want to grow something from seed that will become a lovely green plant, and it will be your project it to keep it alive. You may not feel you have a green thumb, so this task could be a challenge for you, but if you don't have success, try again.

I recommend for this project that set yourself up for success: get new seeds and good soil then put the plant near a window for good light and care for it as carefully as God would want you to care for your heart. You will learn about waiting and being still as you can't dig up the precious seed each day to see how it is doing as that will lead to failure. Same with our hearts. We need to be patient, to wait, and to rest in God's love and care.

As the seed begins to sprout, notice its beauty even in its small and vulnerable state. This is the same as your heart. It was created by the same God who shines light on you. Your heart is precious, so take care of it as well.

Now back to the plant. If you planted a bean seed and there is any chance, it would be ready to put outside to produce fruit go for it. Then you will enjoy a meal that includes fresh produce. If you are in midwinter, please don't freeze the poor plant but see how you can maintain it or grow a few others for company.

 Tips for caregivers

1) Take some time to reflect on the progress made on the journey by the one you walk with. Write a card that could include some stages of growth you have seen. They could be things such as the following:

    i.   more able to share,
    ii. willingness to carry on in the journey,
    iii. progress in self-learning,
    iv. care for self,
    v.   wisdom, and
    vi. patience.

2) Maybe you can ponder how journeying with someone has made positive changes in your life. What have you learned? How have you changed? Why do you think God has called you to this heart? Take that time to ponder about your own journey and you could share that when you feel it is appropriate.

3) Continue to pray. Even when all seem still and quiet, it could also mean a drawing away from people. Keep them involved and connected even in times of rest.

Chapter 8

Masked Molly
Would Anyone Accept Me?

> Psalm 62:5–7
> *"Find rest, O my soul, in God alone;*
> *my hope comes from him*
> *He alone is my rock and my salvation;*
> *he is my fortress;* ***I will not be shaken.***
> *My salvation and my honor depend on God;*
> *he is my mighty rock, my refuge."*

How can one integrate back into society after a huge emotional upheaval? It is difficult for sure. The more you can keep regular life going on during the process, the easier to assimilate back after a break. You will face the need for a conscious transition in the healing journey. The trauma set you heart and mind on a different course—a detour of sorts—but eventually you will need to find the main path of your life once again. This has challenges of its own.

Fear
Fear paralyzes the spirit and soul of man.
It comes from bad experience . . .
The new born baby does not have fear.
Their eyes are curious, soaking up the world around.
Processing the brain for future use.

Fear comes from loss of peace and security.
Fear comes from loss of personal boundaries.
Fear comes from abuse: mental, emotional, physical, sexual.

Fear changes one.
Fear is the opposite of love.
"Love casts out fear"
What does this say for those who have crazy fear?

Does God not love them?
Do people not truly love them?
Do they not love themselves?
Do they not actually know love?
Do they need their love rekindled by humans to sense God's
love?
Does anyone truly know love?
God is our best role model of love.

The issue with taking mental health leaves from work is you can feel as though everyone is suspicious! "Why was ——— away for two weeks of sick leave as they look just fine" is the question that may roam through heart and mind for you. They may care about you and never think such things, but questions still rattle around in your head.

I remember when my mom died, I felt as if I had been transported into a new reality. Shock changes you; it shakes you to the core, and you see things in a much different light or may be even darkness.

After any major trauma strikes, you are left feeling less confident in the tasks that should be habitual. When your self-esteem has been shrunk through abuse, you develop fears you may not have had before: fears that people will hurt you, fears that people will not accept you now that you carry the shame and stigma of being abused, and fears that you are no longer good enough. I went through this, so I understand it mentally, but it is also a struggle to believe what an impact this has made in my life. I consider myself smart, so why can't my mind change my heart into believing I am okay? The heart is a tricky thing to understand. I continue to invest time to sort mine out.

Fear interferes with reality. That is my profound writing phrase of the day. I have long read of people who are paranoid and who have crazy reactions to fears. There are so many. According to a recent website posting, the top few phobias are

---

Figure 8:1 Top fears, as listed by http://www.fearof.net/[29]

---

1. Arachnophobia—The fear of spiders affects women four times more (48% women and 12% men).
2. Ophidiophobia—The fear of snakes. Phobics avoid certain cities because they have more snakes.
3. Acrophobia—The fear of heights. Five percent of the general population suffer from this phobia.
4. Agoraphobia—The fear of open or crowded spaces. People with this fear often won't leave home.
5. Cynophobia—The fear of dogs. This includes everything from small Poodles to large Great Danes.
6. Astraphobia—The fear of thunder/lightning aka brontophobia, tonitrophobia, ceraunophobia.
7. Claustrophobia—The fear of small spaces like elevators, small rooms and other enclosed spaces.
8. Mysophobia—The fear of germs. It is also rightly termed as germophobia or bacterophobia.
9. Aerophobia—The fear of flying. 25 million Americans share a fear of flying.
10. Trypophobia—The fear of holes is an unusual but pretty common phobia.

11. Carcinophobia—The fear of cancer. People with this develop extreme diets.
12. Thanatophobia—The fear of death. Even talking about death can be hard.
13. Glossophobia—The fear of public speaking. Not being able to do speeches.
14. Monophobia—The fear of being alone. Even while eating and/or sleeping.

For those of you who have some of these fears, I am sorry. I do understand fears that do not seem rational but are so intensely real they keep you up at night. My fears were not spiders, or heights, or small spaces. I don't think I have any phobias, but some triggers that affect me in similar way that you will read about. My fears have been things I cannot see.

When I think back to my childhood, I remember how I liked to hide. I had three favorite spots: 1) the closet in my bedroom once we wired with a light; 2) a place in the backyard against a fence and protected by trees where I could see all that happened on the home front and many of the neighbors as well; and 3) the attic of the small playhouse I had as a child. It was a very tight squeeze for sure, but that meant no adults would fit. It is interesting to me that I felt safer in spots that were closed in. For me, these spots were like my little fortresses where I felt safe. The Psalm chosen for this chapter is a reminder that we need a safe place where we can go and not be afraid. We need someone much bigger than us to carry our fears. We need hope to carry on; to emerge from sorrow, pain, and shame; and reconnect with the outside world. Trusting in God is a very important step in this process.

Before you read the short devotional thought on Psalm 62, I suggest you take a breather and put the book aside. Find a comfy spot in your house or yard, and with paper and pencil, make a list of the things you feel scared about. I suggest paper and pen to change it up from electronics.

Take some time now, and then come on back . . .

Psalm 62:5–7

He alone is my rock and my salvation;
*He is my fortress, **I will not be shaken**.*

I have greatly enjoyed the worship of Paul Baloche. He is humble yet stands tall in Christ as a great worship leader in the contemporary praise music context. His wife wrote the text and music for "Shaken," which is on Paul's album *Glorious* released in 2009. In my first listening of the CD, I repeated this song over and over. Scripture says we will not be shaken, yet this song says we will be, but we will make it through. The text of this Baloche song shed new light on my question as to how body and mind can shake. In this shaking, there is a purpose, and despite all I can rest in my Lord who is the fortress. "Everything that can be will be shaken." It is needed for healing, and I can see that in hindsight.

Shaken[30]
Only a spotless lamb
For a Sinner's soul
You gave me a heart of flesh
For a heart of stone
You brought me down to my knees
When I was full of pride
And took away all the places
I could hide
Those you love you will chasten

Everything that can be will be shaken
Everything that can be will be shaken
And only you remain
Only you remain

Wherever my treasure is
There my heart will be
I'm fixing my eyes on things
In the heavenlies

When everything is said and done
And swept away
I wanna be by your side
In eternity
Those you love you will chasten

No suffering for the moment
Is pleasant but it brings forth
The peaceful fruit of righteousness
Jesus my righteousness

Only you remain
Only you remain

With the image of shaking, I think of gold panners sifting and shaking their way through dirt and mud to find the beautiful and shiny specks of true value. So it is with us. We need to have the dust and dirt removed so that we can see clearly what we have and then what we need to do. Our souls are precious, and we need to find the treasure within. God may be shaking you, but it is for good reason. To the end of the journey God walks with you.

God is our refuge and strength. He created the world and everything in it. He controls the universe which we learn is vaster that we could ever imagine. He knows, He cares, and He will be there for you. **God will not let you be shaken past what you can tolerate.**

Verse 5 of this Psalm, which is an echo of sorts of verse one, speaks about finding rest in God alone. If you are like most sufferers of abuse or other PTSD, sleep and rest are difficult when they weren't prior to either the incident or stress healing from the incident. Just as fear and love are opposites, I suggest that fear and rest are also opposites. If you are afraid, your body begins to work in fight or flight and there is no rest available. Recovering from fears is not an easy job. To do it, one must trust and love. To trust a God who you cannot see or hug is a difficult step but very important. Then in time you will need to build trust with others in your life so that feel you can be accepted and loved and fit back into what I will call regular life again. It can happen, but again we need to wait and be patient.

Prayer

Lord, help me to find rest in you. I give you the things of my life which have been shaken and pray that you take them away and create within me something beautiful. You alone are my fortress, so help me to hide with you when I am afraid as you will protect me physically, mentally, and spiritually. Thank you for caring for me. Teach me to better care for myself and feel safe. Amen.

Chapter End Projects
---

1) Let's go back to the project suggested a few pages earlier and do some more work with it. *(Besides if you were like me when reading a new book, you would have just sailed through that without doing it. I get it as I was always in a hurry to find answers without even getting all the questions sorted out.)*

So find a comfortable spot in your house or yard, and with paper and pencil, make (or continue to make) a list of the things you feel scared about. Then ask yourself if there is any reason this fear developed. You may not have answers for that question for your fears, and don't worry about it. You may never know the reasons, which is okay. Some answers may come in time as you continue to learn more about yourself and how you respond to various issues presented to you with your heightened awareness. I am also not asking here for you to fix your fears! Just be aware of them and that can bring a sense of peace to you without taking any risks.

2) This might also be a good time to share with a safe person at work or in your usual circles what you have been going through. This could be an instructor, a boss, an assistant, an on-site counselor, a friend, or someone with whom you feel safe. One of the things mental struggles cause is a tendency to cover up and hide. Being able to share your situation, even if somewhat vaguely, will be helpful for you. Remember, most countries will not allow someone to be fired because of illness, may it be mental, physical, or spiritual. If you are fearful at that thought, then go to someone whom you pay not to talk about your situation with anyone; they could be a psychologist or even a lawyer. At least the secrets, along with your fears, can get out a tiny bit. I have spoken about the fact that this inner child Molly seemed to have been locked in a trunk in my heart, and while she was there I carried on with life unaware. Sharing

and talking can be like providing a breathing hole for your inner child, and the better your inner child does, the better you will do as well.

 Tips for caregivers

1) What fears do you think your friend has? How can you help with that? It is possible that your sharing of your fears in life could help them share as well. Remember you are in a servant role though. Imagine you are part of the technical crew for a large theater production and your role is to have everything in place for support. In the theater, it can be costumes, lights, microphone checks, or sound cues. To assist someone else, it can be to go with them, provide some tips, or be a role model. You do not want, however, to turn the spotlight onto yourself but rather provide a sense of courage to the other.

2) You may not be able to share the work you are doing with others in your life, but maybe you can provide some hints to explain where you have been. If you have called your friend once a day that has taken time away from other things and people, you can share you came alongside someone as a mentor through a struggle. That is quite reasonable to share.

PHASE TWO

Molly Wasn't Finished Yet!

Chapter 9

Morose Molly
Why Am I Going through This Again?

Psalm 55:1–8

"Listen to my prayer, O God,
do not ignore my plea;
hear me and answer me.
My thoughts trouble me and I am distraught
at the voice of the enemy,
at the stares of the wicked;
for they bring down suffering upon me
and revile me in their anger.
My heart is in anguish within me;
the terrors of death assail me.
Fear and trembling have beset me;
horror has overwhelmed me.
I said, "Oh, that I had the wings of a dove!
I would fly away and be at rest—
I would flee far away
and stay in the desert;
I would hurry to my place of shelter,
far away from tempest and storm."

> Psalm 69:1–3
> "Save me, O God.
> for the waters have come up to my neck.
> I sink in the miry depths,
> where there is no foothold.
> I have come into the deep waters;
> the floods engulf me.
> I am worn out calling for help;
> my throat is parched.
> My eyes fail, looking for my God."

The brain is our IQ center and is the logic base for functioning. Many people are quick thinkers but struggle with memory—that is my experience. Despite humankind's efforts to solve the challenge of how gray matter works, it is thus far and will most likely be the last organ of the human body to be understood. With neuroimaging being a new tool for attempting to map the brain, there is potential for more understanding of the brain, but the complexities are vast.

There are more questions than answers for the mind. This is a list I have been working on for years:

- How is it that some people remember everything? We have learned about different learning styles; some memorize at sight, some by feel, some need to hear repetitively to recall.
- How is it that some people can memorize full encyclopedias of information yet have no practical sense with regard to day-to-day life?
- How does the mind store information? Then, how are we able to tap the information once we have made our best attempt to store the information?
- How is it that we forget? Recall is even more difficult when there is trauma involved.
- How can we try to forget when we can't seem to flush the mind of difficult events and situations? Is there a delete button somewhere?
- Where is the easy button to solving issues of the mind?

- How are IQ and EQ related? (IQ is intelligence quotient, while EQ is emotional quotient.)
- Why can one have a high IQ but a poor memory?
- How could everyone seem to know so many answers on the TV show *Jeopardy*?

This chapter overviews the complexities and issues Molly and her adult have had to face. All seemed resolved, life was going well, Molly seemed content . . . I destroyed all the journals that revealed the dark time of my life. I gave away all the books that I had read with intensity as I tried to solve the mysteries of the past and how they had invaded my present. Everything was calm for about fifteen years. Things were going quite well: job, friends, vacations, and family.

During the fall of 2011, the cage began to rattle again (and in fact much worse than ever before). I was triggered by situations of blatant dishonesty by two males in positions of authority. I struggled with how they could get away with cheating. I wondered why no one seemed to care enough to do anything. Are we afraid to stand up for truth, honesty, and integrity? And why does this bother me so much? Two different males in leadership roles who lack a spine and are content to cheat in professions where they are expected to be role models; this was more than Molly could bear. She had been quiet, and though these weren't situations of sexual abuse, the dishonesty factor seemed to be enough to stir Molly's anger and sorrow.

Once again, this new stretch of Molly struggle began with lack of sleep. Molly would wake me up at two o'clock. I could not recall any event for this other than seeing males in leadership being dishonest. I slept about two or three hours a night for months again.

Traumatic memories are processed differently than ordinary memories. During a traumatic experience, our brain is firing off signals that tell our body it's time for "fight, flight, or freeze," the three ways in which we instinctively respond to a threat. To put it simply, our brain experiences an overload of chemicals. According to an article in the August

2006 International Journal of Neuropsychiatric Medicine, "This results in a failure to organize the traumatic event into a coherent, verbally represented narrative." Traumatic memories can be intrusive—we might be unable to quit thinking about them. Or we might forget all or part of the traumatic event, at least for a period of time.[31]

Fight or flight or freeze. I never experienced freeze, and I can't imagine it but it is a real response. Many abused persons experience a flight of sorts. The trauma of the event forces the memory into shut down. The subconscious blocks out pain; it forgets for the survival of the present, but these memories come back to you. There are many variables such as a) intensity of the abuse, b) the higher the level of trust that was violated, c) the age of the victim, and d) the recurrence of the abuse.

Memories can somehow be thrust into the deep subconscious. The trauma can also sit at the edge of the memory so close to coming out that the entire present is distracted. Molly is in that category of intensity at this section of the story. She once again rattles and shakes in the body and mind of a stable, bright adult who must work emotionally above and beyond to stay functioning.

What are these memory experiences? There are many and here listed are the ones I have experienced:

A) Nightmares, where all is so real: seeing the abuser's face, real situations, and overwhelming fear. I often woke up totally stressed but not often aware of what it was I had been dreaming.

B) Flashbacks. These are like PowerPoint slides that slip across the mind and usually at inopportune moments! These often appear as one slide across the screen of the moment that disrupts everything but moves too fast to absorb the information. I felt like an audience member at a presentation wanting to request the slide be backed up so I could absorb what was on it.

C)   Panic attacks, breaking into what seems like a body wave of emotion that leaves one unable to cope. Heightened heart rate, sweating, a feeling of disassociation. Not sure how to even describe but many of you will have had similar experiences. Phase two of Molly even required Ativan occasionally. Am I losing it? As this chapter asks, is Molly morose? Is she coming apart at the seams?

D)   Physical responses. The first few attempts to talk about my abuse was accompanied by what is normally an odd response: the overwhelming need to vomit. I am not anorexic and have never been able to throw up on demand or in a situation. Not anymore. Say too much, which challenges Molly's level of safety, and the stomach rejects the process and all food it has taken in.

E)   Hyperarousal. This was a challenging response. Who wants to admit that they are a survivor of intense abuse and that when they think about it at times they have a sexual response? Did I enjoy it? No, but the small body of Molly was aroused, and this is a strong negative feeling and emotion. It too gets triggered somehow through memory, and this itself brings a sense of shame to me. As I did more reading in my journey, I discovered this was quite common:

When people remember an ordinary event, they do not also relive the physical sensations, emotions, images, smells, or sounds associated with that event. In contrast, when people fully recall their traumas, they 'have' the experience: They are engulfed by the sensory or emotional elements of the past.[32] (van der Kolk)

I couldn't understand, but had to accept, that this emotional roller coaster was triggering many points of mind and body. It has been a relief to read about other people's experiences and know that is not unusual. A book I have quoted from a lot on trauma and the brain states,

> *Trauma is much more than a story about something that happened long ago. The emotions and physical sensations that were imprinted during trauma are experienced not as memories but as disruptive physical reactions in the present.*[33] (van der Kolk)

F) Emotional response. Overwhelming need to just cry. Did Molly and her adult not grieve? Why is it so easy to cry? Can the eyes ever run out of tears? I know I have been triggered to tears in movies and TV shows to the point I quit going to the movie theater as I was laughed at for crying at everything. The movies I watched were usually happy memories or positive intimate moments of love, and the tears would start to roll down my cheeks. I have taken a liking to murder mysteries on TV as a replacement to most other shows. Death doesn't trigger for me, and I seem to like it when the bad guy/gal gets caught in the end. Maybe I could live vicariously through that concept that my abusers would pay in the end; if not in this world, then in the next through what I see as God's judgment of condemnation for these serious crimes against humankind.

These feelings and responses all came back in 2011 as signals that suggest a more intense hiding of the pain that has not yet been resolved. Yikes. How could I endure a phase two, when phase one emptied me of emotional and physical energy?

Ah, that's it! I had dealt with all I could in 1996 and 1997. I had seen the most my mind was willing to release, and the most my broken heart could have imagined. I became comfortable and had possibly shut the lid of the trunk with Molly still inside where she had been before. I started a journal in 2011 where her adult and Molly wrote letters to each other. I choose a nice new book, which had a dedication page, and I wrote the following:

> "This book is dedicated to Molly. May I get to
> know her and love her for who she is!"

How profound in retrospection. I had learned about Molly previously but did not treat her as an accepted part of me. Learning to accept Molly was required.

I chuckled as I reviewed some of my journal entries. I had drawn a picture of a trunk where I imagined Molly was hiding. It does **not** resemble a trunk but more of a coffin. Oops. True I am not someone you would want on your Pictionary team, but I didn't want to kill Molly. She was and is part of me. At times, she was the embarrassing child you wish was invisible, but she was just a child and her heart was hurt. Well, Molly was back pounding on the walls of the trunk/coffin and she wants equal rights.

> Molly says,
>
> *You need to accept me. You may have heard me, but you stuffed me . . . I embarrass you. You can't talk about me, you can't let me out to experience the world you live in. I can't reach out to others to help them because you can't be honest. Why can't you accept me? When will you allow Molly to integrate with her adult? What is my purpose in life? All you think about is your purpose. You want to look right, say the right things, be accepted by others, but in doing so you reject me. Don't I have value? Adult, when will you accept Molly? I am the victim, and you continue to victimize me by shutting me in the trunk of your heart . . . in the safe place under lock and key. I want out . . . I want to have a happy childhood. Is it too late for fun, for healing? I want to try! Please, adult, help me!"*

Oh my, that is quite the message to hear. Maybe Molly isn't morose after all although it feels like it. Maybe her pain is indeed more than I can understand. More than I can recall. More than I can carry.

> *The subconscious*
> *We are more complicated than we can imagine.*
> *The subconscious which we can't access . . .*
> *Memories that somehow get locked in . . .*
>
> *Yet these memories rattle and shake from the inside.*
> *They stir in dreams*
> *They stir in waking.*
> *What are the triggers?*
> *How deep must one travel to access the subconscious?*
> *Does one arrive back to reality safely?*
> *Does the fear of the unknown hamper the journey?*
>
> *Lord, bring to light that which I must know to proceed.*
> *Open the subconscious and allow out what needs to be healed.*
> *Create in me a new heart purified of the negative.*
> *Heal that which I don't know, and assist me with what I do know.*

Psalm 55:1–8 and Psalm 69:1–3

This reflection was written in October 2016 when Hurricane Matthew has completed its devastation through Haiti all the way up to South Carolina. It was quite the storm with an impact as far north as the Canadian east coast. Wind, water, flash floods, and sea wall were destroyed. Tidal waves had left many communities without power, drinking water, trees. In Haiti, many have lost their homes. Nothing like a level 4 hurricane to create turmoil. In this level of storm, people and structures are vulnerable. Figuratively those who have been abused also experience an inner hurricane of sorts. We have a flood of emotions wash over us. At times we feel as though we are drowning in shame, and often these come at an unexpected time much like a sea wall wave in a hurricane.

In the church, we are encouraged to look right and to behave right. I think we often check our emotions at the door just like we might check a coat at the theater. We do this I think to feel better about ourselves. I know I am guilty of doing it. I have had bad days when the standard line of "I'm good thanks, how about you" automatically responds to questions of how I am doing. It is like we are preprogrammed.

In both Psalm readings, the psalmist is in agony. Take a moment and go back and read them at the start of this chapter. I am sure in this state the author might have driven his friends and his family crazy with anguish. But stuffing it and pretending it is not there doesn't help. We are called to cast our cares to God mentioned later in Psalm 55 than the passage I chose to look at.

If we don't know what our cares are, how can we cast them to God? How can we give away what we can't acknowledge? We must feel those burdens. We can't check them at the door or delete them with the quick touch of a handy delete button on the computer. We, like the psalmist, need to learn of the sorrows and then can give them away to recover.

I agree with the sentiment of Psalm 55:7–8 that it would be nice to fly away as a dove and find a spot that is safe from storm and worry. It is interesting that the bird chosen here is the dove. Often the eagle is used (Isaiah 40:31) as it is a large bird that can soar above all. It catches a breeze and puts out its wings and flies. It does less well, apparently, without wind but it is so majestic!

The dove is a bird that flaps its wings like crazy to get anywhere. No soaring for that bird. In the New Testament, the dove is depicted as the bird from heaven which flies down and settles on Jesus when Jesus is baptized. A voice from heaven then says, "*This is my son in whom I delight*" (Luke 3:22). The dove is the symbol for the Holy Spirit in our churches, and is also used as a sign of peace.

Why did the psalmist choose a dove over an eagle? Maybe because of its ability to fly away in any weather and be small enough to hide? I am tempted to desire the ability to soar like the eagle, but after reflection, I too would probably choose a dove. The dove is a beautiful white which reflects a purity, and its strong connection to peace (olive branch stories) is a draw for my heart. Noah used the dove to see if the storm God sent was complete. When the dove returned with an olive branch, Noah knew the time to leave the boat was coming soon. We all want storms to be done soon! When the dove didn't return after another flight practice, all were ready to leave the ark!

Based on the story of the dove returning with an olive branch, it would be interesting to ponder how you may know when your flood is complete. When will you know the storm has ceased in your life? Reflect on that when you are able. May your mind take you to the future and the release from the storm. May you have hope that the storm will indeed end. The period of waiting may indeed be long, but there is an end to every terrible storm! When the storm subsides, you will be able to pause, reflect, and rebuild your life as needed.

Prayer (from Psalm 55)
"Listen to my prayer, O God,
do not ignore my plea;
hear me and answer me.
My thoughts trouble me, and I am distraught.
My heart is in anguish within me;
the terrors of death assail me.
Fear and trembling have beset me;
horror has overwhelmed me.
I said, "Oh, that I had the wings of a dove!

I would fly away and be at rest—
I would flee far away
and stay in the desert;
I would hurry to my place of shelter,
far away from tempest and storm."
Amen.

Chapter End Projects

There will be stages and phases of healing. There will be times you are great and others where you might be catching up with yourself. However, the more you search and continue to travel, the easier things will get. I am sorry there is no guide book for life that contains events and answers to all your questions. The closest travel guide or map we have is the Bible. However, it contains few specifics to our individual situations but only a reminder to hold on to God, and He will be faithful.

I will share with you now a new memory that came to be while I have been writing this book. I am not sure why it also was not in my retrievable memory earlier, but I remember a neighborhood boy coming over to play. I knew some of his family, but he and I had never played. His type of play was in the dark and the corner of our rumpus room. That I remember well. It didn't feel good. Things being stuck here and there. He didn't stay long. I watched him leave through the back door, down the long sidewalk, and through the back gate until he was out of sight as headed to his home. He never came again that I can recall, and I was glad.

1) Your project is to take some time to search your heart and mind for other things. I know in my youth a church leader used to talk about cleaning the various rooms of your heart. Little did I know I had so much mess there. I never used a flashlight in my cleaning obviously! In fact, to this day I learn more about myself and my response to things on my journey.

2) Make some lists of other people you know of who have struggled with depression or addiction or was abused. This isn't a contest but look at that list and know there is hope for you. You should see there are many that have bleak pasts who have done amazing things. I include some stories in chapter 15, but for now ponder in your own heart. You are not alone. Many have thoughts that trouble them and they

struggle each day. The good thing about most challenges we face is there is recovery possible with patience and time. If you have lost a limb, no prosthesis will bring actual healing but a way to cope. You can heal from trauma. Others have. Remember you are not crazy!

 Tips for caregivers

1) Be patient.
2) Keep being patient.
3) Always be patient and loving.
4) For many, the hurts have been tucked deep within and have impacted many things. As the healing journey continues, there will be what seems like earthquakes and tornados. Be faithful and accepting. That is the gift needed most in the journey. If someone had told me I was too slow, I would have been crushed. I felt too slow, but I needed others to be patient.
5) Keep praying. God is the master healer, and it is beyond our ability.

Chapter 10

Molly's Mesh
Who Can Help Me?

> Psalm 25:20
> *"Guard my life and rescue me;*
> *let me not be put to shame,*
> *for I take refuge in you."*
>
> Psalm 73:2–5
> *"But as for me, my foot had almost slipped;*
> *I nearly lost my foothold.*
> *For I envied the arrogant*
> *when I saw the prosperity of the wicked.*
> *They have no struggles;*
> *their bodies are healthy and strong.*
> *They are free from the burdens common to man;*
> *they are not plagued by human ills."*

As the psalmist has suggested, it is easy for us to look at the lives of others and say, "They have no struggles," but how do we know?

The last chapter ended with the realization that Molly's pain is more intense than I could either imagine or cope with. I needed help—I needed a support system. I had obviously not been able to "cure" Molly myself. I had been impatient with her. I had hoped God would instantly heal me, bring me a new life, and heal memories. I had prayed, I had begged, and I had become impatient. Like the psalmist, I too am jealous of those who seem to have no struggles. Everyone seems so well put together, and I am coming apart at the seams. I envy others and their happy lives, living in the present and dreaming of the future, while I wade through the mire and mud of the past. Any present joy can be sideswiped by a flashback and by what seems like irrational fear. If one in four females have been abused, how can they be so put together? How could they work this all through so much better than I? What is wrong with me? Will Molly ever pull it together?

Okay . . . so I needed help. It was too big a burden for me. A little internet research to find some recent books to order. An online newsletter service? Well, okay. No one should be able to find me out through that and I can grow in my knowledge and eventually my heart will be changed, right?

Most authors talk about how they needed to tell their story to others and in so doing to verbalize their thoughts. For that, I need a support team. How does one find a support team to deal with heavy heart issues? I had usually been considered the caregiver person. I give to others. How can I learn to take? How can I even ask?

For those that have been abused, issues of trust are daunting. Our boundaries have been invaded, and for many it is by people they knew . . . people they trusted and saw as friends. Abuse is a secret society of sorts; it is hard to admit. Most people don't want to talk about these things, but acceptance of self comes through being willing to accept the past and ask for help in sharing the load.

I believe the deepest change in us occurs as we remain faithful, open, and engaged in relationship. (Dr. Dan Allender)[34]

I was not in a rush to find my support team this time around. I needed to be careful as a church family had rejected me before. You also need to be careful in finding a support team. A mistake when the heart is fragile could be too much to bear. Jesus spoke of sharing the load in Matthew 11:28–30:

> *Come to me, all you who are weary and burdened and I will give you rest. Take my yoke upon you and learn from me, for I am gentle and humble in heart, and you will find rest for your souls. For my yoke is easy and my burden is light.*

That is the scripture I wanted to claim: rest for my soul. Inability to sleep is one huge sign of unresolved conflict, and the exhaustion of living in the present while sifting through the past is reason for a desperate call for rest. We have a role, though; it doesn't just happen. We must actively take the yoke Jesus offers us. It is our job. And of course, we need to know that coming to a place of rest is not instant. Bummer!

Jesus never said we would be without hardship, and the psalmist doesn't either but admits he is jealous. What we have through the work of Christ on the cross and through our baptism is the Holy Spirit, who is introduced to us as the comforter and a source of power. By the Holy Spirit we have been adapted into a new body with Christ as the head. Believers are united in service and are to be a support to each other.

We are unfamiliar with the concept of a yoke as most of us are city dwellers and don't see the rustic use of a yoke in animals. The yoke in a sense does govern or train an animal, but the most important concept is two animals share the load and make the task much easier. It is like as instant mentorship program!

If we take up the yoke with Jesus, we not only make a commitment to see the work through but also to see through His eyes as the master teacher and the one who says His yoke is easy. He will carry the weight of our hearts once we give them over . . . once we are willing to work with Him.

So the most important member of any person's support team is God, and the gift given to each of us of the Holy Spirit who gives us both the power and the gifts to press on. Giving over all the pain and anguish in our hearts at foot of the cross and leaving them there for Jesus to heal is a daily process. I am comfortable with my own pain; after all, I have had it for years. If I leave it at the cross, will anyone see it? Will anyone see me leaving it there? We can become content in our struggle, so much so that the cure may not seem worth it. It is. Do hang in there!

Back to the opening of the psalm: *"Guard my life and rescue me."* Our creator will rescue us. He stands at the door and knocks at the door of our hearts. He knocks right at the door of our pain and shame. We need to take the initiative to open the door and accept help from our God who knows us better than we know ourselves.

I have been a Christian for many years, and while I sought the Lord for healing, I obviously had more work to do. I felt I could solve this on my own, but I couldn't seem to do it myself, and a few hotline prayers won't cover it either.

The heart of an abuse victim feels very alone. They are afraid and have a shame that most others cannot identify with no matter how hard they might try to empathize. Molly had felt very alone in what I would refer to as phase two. This was probably from her need to express her pain more and try to come to a safe place. Her heart cried for relationships that matter as we live in such a superficial world. Take Facebook as an example, can one really have that many friends? No. We are pretending to be connected. I have heard that in one's lifetime, if you can count true friends on five fingers, you have been fortunate. Friendships take time and energy. It is a commitment. We do have many friendships and connections but only a small group that can serve as a support network.

> *The hand*
> *The hand that heals reaches out to mine*
> *It expresses care and concern.*
> *It warms my heart*
> *It brings life to my brokenness*
> *It recharges hope in mankind*
> *It gives hope to trust again*
> *May this hand not leave too soon . . .*
> *May God's Spirit flow to encourage and heal my brokenness.*

To make it through the struggle of abuse, one does need a support network. I built what I thought was a brilliant one in 2011 with a pastor, a doctor, and two others. The four has dropped to three. I was very sad to be rejected by one member of the team, and this was a significant loss at a vulnerable time. The team members all had different gifts and things they brought to Molly for her process: intelligence and logic, spiritual encouragement, and time to invest when things are tough. I can't thank them enough. To truly hold one's heart as it grieves is a rare gift. I encourage you to ponder carefully who should be on your team. I made an error that did have consequences for me, but I was 75 percent right, and for human friendship statistics for a heavy heart issue that is great. I wouldn't have made it without the network I have, so seek out the friendship of others carefully! I am also grateful that I have been able to help my team members in their crisis moments too.

Traumatized human beings recover in the context of relationships: with families, loved ones, AA meetings, veteran's organizations, religious communities, or professional therapists. The role of relationships is to provide physical and emotional safety, including safety from feeling shamed, admonished, or judged, and to bolster the courage to tolerate fear and process the reality of what has happened. (van der Kolk)[35]

> A friend
> God has sent a soul mate.
> Someone who is
> patient
> accepting
> caring
> gentle
> loving
>
> With her Molly feels
> at rest
> cared for
> willing to try to trust
>
> Thank you Lord for breaking through
> to my heart via my soul sister.
> I thank you for connecting us by heart.
> Bless her for her investment.
> Amen.

I feel that after years of travelling this journey, those who can support the most are those who have walked or are walking a similar journey. Yes, I have said before that **we will be the most important caregivers for ourselves, but we cannot do it all on our own**. We need a small caring network of friends, and they will come in many forms: those who help us do things when we are unable to, those who have time and can walk or sit with us, and those who will support us in life with those things that are a stretch. Of course, walking alongside us is also God as Father, Son, and Holy Spirit. They as trinity are the best comforter package.

While I was in the process of healing, my reading materials have not just been about abuse, but also about a vast array of topics. One book, *Falling Upward*, is about spirituality as we age and the life journey of aging. I found the following quote very meaningful:

Jesus seems to often find love in people who might not have received much love themselves. Perhaps their deep

***longing for it became their capacity to both receive
and give it.***[36] (Richard Rohr ***in*** *Falling Upward*)

Groups of similar souls have an instant bond, which will help each other in the journey no matter where they are. And, the fact that I, and possibly you as well, was not loved well in my childhood does not mean I cannot and do not love as others. More depth in heart does allow for more space to fill with love!

Psalm 73

We are often jealous of the bling people have in their lives, as well as those who have what appears to be no burdens. The sun and rain do continue to fall equally to the faithful and the faithless. With our time on earth we are not treated better than any others. The blessing for our faith and upright living comes after this life when we enter a place where there are no more tears.

The psalmist shares our feelings of frustration and jealousy when he looks outside himself, but then he went to God's sanctuary (v. 17) and has a revelation of how dumb he was (v. 22). He saw himself as one of the pure in heart when he complained his life was tough. Yet, as his poem and song carries on, he realizes he carries this jealousy, which makes his heart contaminated with sinful thoughts. We will never know what goes on in the lives of others as they could be as stuffed as we are at times. We are responsible for ourselves alone: thoughts, feelings, and actions. We alone are accountable for our actions and responses to others.

I need to remember I was created to walk **my** journey through life and not theirs. We do not need to walk alone though. God will walk with all of us who trust Him. Rather than experiencing jealousy of those that seem to have it all together, we would do best to sort out our own hearts before God. It is then we can reach out in honesty and seek true friendships with others.

Many groups are formed to help others through similar struggles: Alcoholics Anonymous, Narcotics Anonymous, Weight Watcher groups, etc. These groups try to support each other and help people see they are not the only ones going through these issues. They create a support team. Members become accountable to each other. Having others walk with you is a great way to release feelings of jealousy and envy as they will understand your story and share their experiences. You may be able to find a support group like this with the help of a therapist. I did not join such a group to support Molly, but I am confident others have benefitted from such a process. But start first with God as your anchor and best friend.

Let's now read from later in Psalm 73 when the writer could turn from the bling of the world that has distracted him to the greatness of God.

Psalm 73:25–28

"Whom have I in Heaven but you?
And being with you, I desire nothing on earth.
My flesh and my heart may fail,
But God is the strength of my heart and my portion forever.
Those who are far from you will perish.
You destroy all who are unfaithful to you.
But as for me, it is good to be near God.
I have made the sovereign Lord my refuge;
I will tell of all your deeds."

Remember that God is indeed the strength of your heart. Stay close to the creator, run after God, and hang on tightly. Paul suggests we "pray without ceasing" (1 Thess. 5:16). May this be something you can develop more in time.

Prayer

Lord, guide me to your side and help me to find friends I can trust and who care about me. May I begin to feel safe with others to share the deepest secrets in my heart. Teach me how to love and be loved, show me how I can accept the care of others and care for myself. On days when my heart and mind are in a muddle, give me your wisdom and strength to carry through. Assist me with the heart transplant I feel I need to recover. When I am able, I too will sing of your help and shine as a light for you. Amen.

Chapter End Projects

1) You need a support system. We all do, but even more so in crisis. I recommend that you **start with prayer**. God will hear you, but in His timing. And He will send who you need and this might not necessarily be who you want but who you need. Pray for wisdom too.

2) **Decide what type of support network you might feel comfortable with**. Do you want to enroll in group therapy, do you want individual counseling, do you want to connect with someone you know has been through a similar situation? There are many options. Knowing the options and what you would feel best with are important for successful completion of the journey.

3) **If you haven't been journaling already consider getting started.** A record of thoughts and ponderings is interesting. It could also help you vocalize thoughts in preparation to share with your support team.

4) Ask one person for starters. Remember you may have some who won't make the entire journey with you. That happens. **Be prepared to forgive those that can't travel your journey**. It could be their own baggage that keeps them at the security check and it may have nothing to do with you and your journey.

5) So, now that you have been presented with some ideas, **find yourself a network** to support you. Keep it small and make sure you feel safe. There is no rush for this important step.

 Tips for caregivers

1) Recognize your role on the support team. Your role may be the encourager, or possibly the challenger, but all must be done in love.

2) Make sure you are not the only one on the team. You will find the task of mentoring long and tiring. If you have others, you too will be stronger. Find others for the support network, or possibly for your own support network. God has blessed us with caring brothers and sisters, and usually all we need do is ask.

Chapter 11

Molly's Maze
How Long?

> Psalm 13:1–2
>
> *"How long, O Lord? Will you forget me forever?*
> *How long will you hide your face from me?*
> *How long must I wrestle with my thoughts*
> *and every day have sorrow in my heart?*
> *How long will my enemy triumph over me?"*

Here we go again. In chapter 2, the question was "**when**," now I have advanced to "**how long**?" Is there any progress in that? Hmm . . . I ponder and decide I have only doubled the length of question from one word to two. Is that an advance or a further delay? I am again in a similar spot! Rats.

Jan 14/12 Journal Entry: *"When will I know I've been healed? Well . . . I am sure God could heal Molly instantly, but I don't see that happening. She's so stuffed, so sad, so lonely—it can overwhelm me."*

It was after this entry that I took a four-and-a-half-year break from writing. I did have other responsibilities as a distraction in the form of a new job, but all stopped with this short paragraph. In that long stretch much healing has occurred thankfully!

Figure 11.1 has an old clock face (not digital), but it is also missing hands to tell the time. This resonates with the idea of how long. Sometimes we must wait. We don't know the present hour and we don't know the goal, so we wait. During this period of waiting, we are often unable to see the actual passing of time in our healing.

Figure 11:1. How long do we wait when we don't know the time then, now, or in the future?

When, oh Lord? I have echoed the thoughts of the psalmist saying, how long O Lord will this journey last? Are you still there?

I am reminded of mistakes made when people struggle with waiting. Remember the story of Moses going up Mount Sinai and fellowshipping with God? We read that to the Israelites, "the glory of the Lord looked like a consuming fire on top of the mountain" (Ex 24:17). Moses was up on that mountain top forty days and nights. That is a long time for sure! And what was he learning up there on the mount with God? Rules about offerings, the ark, the table, the lampstand, the tabernacle, the courtyard, the altar for burnt offerings, priestly garments, the breastplate, the process to ordain priests, incense and anointing oil, the Sabbath, etc.! Moses was doing a crash course of "Being God's People 101" offered by God himself. Meanwhile back on earth, the people were bored and had maybe given up hope of seeing Moses again. They were not waiting well! Granted forty days is a long time to wait for someone and they probably assumed he had been burned up in the consuming fire on the mountain top. It is in not waiting they sin. Along with the second in charge, Aaron, they melt gold into an image of a calf and begin to worship it. Moses comes down after his long crash course in being a leader for God. We don't know for sure, but he is probably tired, hungry, thirsty, and exhausted trying to remember all the rules about how to build things to stay in right relationship with God. Down he comes and he gets so mad with what he sees he breaks the two stone tablets that contain the Ten Commandments, part of the new covenant with God. Oops.

This story of the early Jewish church is an excellent reminder that we need to be content with waiting as there could be a very good reason for it that we are unaware of. How did things go for the calf worshipping crew you may ask? Well, a plague. But God did show his forgiveness to the people, as Moses interceded for them. It is human for all of us to struggle with waiting and being patient. Healing can be years depending on the seriousness of physical or emotional healing. Practice patience! And when you are tired of being patient, try being **more patient**.

> *Tunneling Down*
> *The heart of the abused has been sheltered*
> *Carefully protected away from all further damage.*
> *It is in a deep dry well and it takes a long time to get there.*
> *The process of healing requires much time in the tunnel*
> > *in the dark*
> > *alone*
> > *pondering*
> > *crying.*
>
> *Then it seems one needs to dig even a bit deeper to feel more pain and then again spend more time in the tunnel*
> > *in the dark*
> > *alone*
> > *pondering*
> > *crying.*
>
> *Then more pondering and trying to make it—just to breathe*
>
> *It is a small tunnel;*
> *most likely why the process can be so lonely.*
> *No one else can fully feel the pain with you.*   ...

... Many have a similar experience
yet each one has their own tunnel or cave to process.
The abuse occurred in secret
And it seems in many ways the healing also must occur in secret.
To expect others to crawl into the tunnel with you is too much.
They can be there when you emerge
> *to wipe away the tears*
> *to hold you*
> *to remind you that you have value.*
But it is a journey to the deep that must be traveled with con-
fidence on your own.
The good news:
one can't get lost in the tunnel as there is only one way up to
the top.
The journey is heart-wrenching
and may take considerable time
but the growth and healing it brings
makes for a soul that may once again be free.
Free to have relationship.
> *Free to share again.*
> *Free to be open and not stuffed.*
The journey is hard,
but it is worth all the effort to complete.

Tie for yourself a lifeline at the top and hang on tight.
Bring a head lamp with long battery life to see as best as you can.
And try to have a support team ready each time you come up for air.
They can hold you, love you, and remind you that you are valuable,
something that seems to be essential to hear a lot on this journey!

Psalm 13:1–2

The first two verses of this Psalm echo how long four times all related to the petition that God needs to get busy and rescue David from his misery. He feels God has forgotten him—that God may be playing a spiritual game of hide-and-seek. God doesn't hide from us, but we are quite good at either hiding or not hearing the voice of our creator. As we often see in these poems of the Old Testament, they start very bleak and change quite quickly. Psalm 13 has just six verses: the first four question God, and then a sudden change is made. David says that he will continue to trust in God's unfailing love. It would be great to know what happened in the life of David between total despair in verses one through four and the healing, which even talks of singing for joy. Reading this can make our hearts ache even more as the answer for the sudden change is not given. Did David have some wild herbal tea that changed his disposition? Did a friend wander over and tell David he was being too dramatic? Did ten years lapse between verse four and verse five? Wouldn't you love to know the answer? Me too. It seems like such a shift. From valley to mountaintop in a single breath. Sounds like a helicopter rescue of one's spirit! How does this happen? And why does it happen to David in a short phrase of a poem when it seems to be so long for me? We continue to echo the words "how long" when David speaks of his heart rejoicing and singing. Is all we need to trust?

The maze will take a while to go through. I am reminded of stories of people who climb the big mountains of the world. They prepare themselves by getting in shape, getting used to less oxygen, planning the route, and then take all the items they will need because the big trips—Mount Everest being the supreme challenge—do not have cell phone service or pizza delivery. Things I didn't know before some study was that the climbers often must wait inside small tents for long periods of time partway to the summit for the right weather conditions. Then, unless they have hired a crew of helpers, they often must climb up with some of the gear, park it, and then go back down the mountain to the prior camp as there are too many things to carry in one load. In my naivety, I assumed that mountain climber just went up, but that isn't the case. There are many stops and back tracks to a successful journey which sees the hiker both reach the summit and arrive home. The process depends on so many factors . . . so it is with recovery from trauma. Please read this quote below from an article entitled, "Psychological and Physiological Requirements" with regards to pre-trip preparation:

Perhaps one of the toughest things about climbing a mountain like Everest is keeping motivated for months. Plan to spend a lot of time in your tent, waiting for the opportunity to go higher on the mountain. Be aware that you will probably be socked in by strong weather for at least a period of time, weather can intimidate you and weaken your reserve. You may have climbing mates who get sick, have to descend without you, or worse (heaven forbid) never come back home. At some point you will likely get sick yourself, yet still have to perform. You may be in top physical condition but get struck with something you never expected. Mental fortitude, an ability to roll with whatever comes along, and above all a strong desire to succeed are all vital to your success on a mountain like Everest. (From Body Results Website)[37]

There are many similarities between mountain climbing and the process of healing from trauma: we need to keep motivated to press on in the journey, we need to expect significant time to wait, we must be ready for things to weaken our goals, we may lose friends who can't make the entire journey with us, and we need to be strong enough to press on even when it is too hard. This is not an easy journey we are on. How many times have you driven in a car with young kids who constantly say, "Are we there yet?" barely one hour into an eight-hour drive? No, you may not be there yet, but the good news is that you are pressing on. If you are still in the car and awake, then that is good. You may need to be in neutral or even reverse, but if you see the road and have gas in the tank, you are good! In the mountain climbing preparation quote above they use the phrase 'socked in.' You may be at a point in your journey where you too feel socked in. The clouds are grey and heavy. The wind bitter and cold. You may feel as though the sun will never shine again. Find the faith to hold on to the idea that the sun will indeed return and bring warmth and relief. You can finish the journey but be prepared to be socked in occasionally. Sometimes in your journey you may have to switch gears just to survive the usual days. Think of this story: You haven't cleaned your home for a while and someone phones to say they are stopping in. You have flashbacks of the TV show *Hoarders* as your eyes scan the house. You have sixty minutes to clean. Yes, some areas are clean, but other areas have been made worse by the tossing of items you are trying to hide. (*Please tell me this isn't just my story!*) You have a pleasant visit, but then open the door to your study to find it filled to the brim and your work was just delayed more from having to clean from your cleaning. Just as we try to hide clutter, we also work hard to hide trauma that at times feels as though it is taking over. Don't stuff the pain away as it will come back. Both solving the maze and hiking to Everest takes time and patience.

> *The first great enemy to lasting change is the propensity to turn our eyes away from the wound and pretend things are fine. The work of restoration cannot begin until a problem is fully faced.*
> (Dr. Dan B. Allender)[38]

Prayer

Lord, forgive me. I have tried to jump the cue. I have tried to rush the process. I need to do a full survey and clean of my heart that I might heal fully. I have impeded my healing by trying to take control, but it is my subconscious and my heart that needs to heal. My mind trying to push things along will not help. Give me patience to accept all my heart must deal with. Teach me that rushing through may create more work later. Help me not run away but rather to face the issues head on and trust You as the master healer. Amen.

Chapter End Projects

1) "Molly's Maze" is the title of this chapter. Life brings us many things and they often come in puzzle form. I know of many families that solve puzzles over the Christmas break as they are a fun group project and are indoors when the weather is often frightful over the bleak midwinter holiday season. Solving puzzles is fun. Some people like Sudoku number puzzles, or word search puzzles, or crosswords. I like the old-fashioned puzzle with its one thousand pieces of many shapes and colors. There is something nice about sorting the pieces and finding spots for them all. While you wait for God and for healing, try some other puzzles to pass the time and give you a project that gives you something new to ponder. These puzzles will give you hope that your internal puzzles may also resolve.

2) Take some time to do a full survey of your heart. Pretend that there was a magic wand to heal everything you have on a list and then get started making the list. It may be very long but don't worry about that. Just try to find things within the muddle and maze of life that you would like sorted out. This project could take months or minutes depending on how much pondering you have done to this point. It is important. It is with having the list and facing the issues that you can face them head on and sort through them. I had done enough stuffing. It was on to full turkey now! ☺ I pray the same will be with you. When you are discouraged, remember the quote by Allender about restoration coming when you see the problems.

3) Continue to pray. Pray for God's guidance and His healing. Place your trust in him. He will see you through your journey.

Tips for caregivers

1) Encourage your friends to carry on. We all must grow, and if we stop growing, we experience a spiritual death of sorts.
2) Make sure there is always gas in the tank for yourself and the one you are helping as the journey carries on. This includes rest, food, exercise, vacation time, socials, and quiet pondering time.

Chapter 12

Molly's Mystery
Where Is God in the Confusion?

Psalm 42

As the deer pants for streams of water, so
my soul pants for you, O God.
My soul thirsts for God, for the living God.
When can I go, and meet with God?
My tears have been my food day and night,
*while men say to me all day long, "**Where is your God**?"*
These things I remember as I pour out my soul:
how I used to go with the multitude,
leading the procession to the house of God,
with shouts of joy and thanksgiving among the festive throng.
Why are you downcast, O my soul?
Why so disturbed within me?
Put your hope in God, for I will yet praise him,
my Saviour and my God.
My soul is downcast within me; therefore, I will remember you
from the land of the Jordan, the heights of
Hermon—from Mount Mizar.
Deep calls to deep in the roar of your waterfalls;
all your waves and breakers have swept over me.
By day the Lord directs his love, at night his song is with me—
a prayer to the God of my life.

> *I say to God my Rock, "Why have you forgotten me?*
> *Why must I go about mourning, oppressed by the enemy?"*
> *My bones suffer mortal agony as my foes taunt me,*
> *saying to me all day long, **"Where is your God?"***
> ***Why are you downcast, O my soul?***
> ***Why so disturbed within me? Put your hope in God,***
> ***for I will yet praise him, my Saviour and my God.***

In an upcoming chapter, I add in a picture of an onion and refer to layers of understanding and memories. In this chapter, I look at my own layers. You and I will often have a cover story for the things we feel or respond to. I would call this cover story a short version of what is going on or a rational interpretation of things we can't understand.

An easy first example to illustrate for my reader is the writing of this book. Here I am in my year off, and when I tell someone I am writing a book, they want the details . . . but I am hesitant to open up about my story in a short, twenty-second answer. I am protecting my heart. I am not lying to say the book is about the book of Psalms and the journey of life, but I need way more time and a feeling of safety to tell the story of pain and shame and my recovery process.

Even years later traumatized people often have enormous difficulty telling other people what has happened to them.[39]

We need to protect our hearts and our story. For myself, I am just beginning to move outside the small circle of my support system. Telling some others, doing a TED-style talk at church, asking a group of people to read the book draft. There is tremendous risk to the already fragile heart. One doesn't want to be rejected.

I have had several cover story layers as I look back, and I wasn't aware of all of them at the start. The outer layers tended to be easier to share, but as I moved inward to the kernel of the abuse at the very core, it has been very difficult to share. Molly never appeared fully until the final layer was revealed. I have set these up in Fig 12:1 as a countdown of sorts. At times, these may have overlapped or changed, but I would say these were my layers of understanding and awareness:

Figure 12:1 Molly's and her adult's trigger and travels

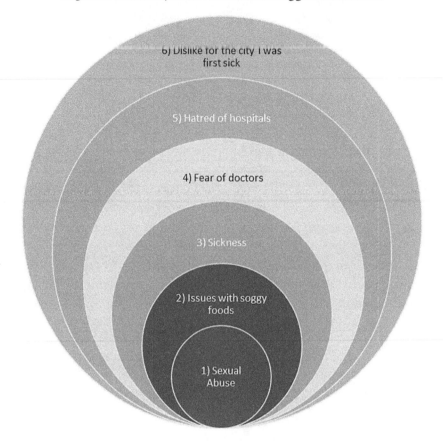

6) The City

The city where I was first sick I disliked even though it wasn't the city's fault. Granted the mosquito lived there, which brought my initial illness, but I somehow linked my issues to that place. I left there with my family when I was five to a city about 250 kilometers north. When I drove through my city of birth, however, I would usually get stressed. I thought to myself that it was because of my tough childhood illness there.

5) Hatred of Hospitals

The smell of hospitals gets me. I am not sure what it is, but doing hospital visits even in the present is hard for me. I must talk myself into it. I also do better if I have someone else with me. I can still easily panic. A few years ago, I went to see the husband of a close friend. He was unfortunately at the same hospital my sexual abuse occurred at, although it has been rebuilt and looks nothing like the old version. My fight/flight sensors were on overdrive. As we were leaving, the elevator descended and literally dropped a few floors to the basement. We had pushed the main floor, but the elevator clunked down to the basement. Here we were stuck between floors. The elevator, after its sudden drop, was bumping along and finally made it back up to the reception level rather than being bottomed out. The windows were glass, and I was thrilled to see main floor; I bolted out of the elevator straight to the bathroom. The friend I was with went to tell the information desk of the elevator's drop, and I had instant diarrhea and a sweating/panic spell. I don't use bathrooms in public places unless it is a near-death experience or there is no option. This fight/flight nervous tendency that can even affect bowels has been studied and is quite a common response to flashbacks and stress.[40] Will going to the hospital myself or to visit others be easier with time? I am not sure. I think it is better. At least I understand the issues and have a better chance of knowing that the past and present are different!

4) Fear of Doctors

I have always distrusted doctors. Granted many are smart and would never hurt me, but I will do anything I can to avoid going to a clinic. I recently told someone I think I would prefer to die of cancer rather than treat it; this might change if I were faced with this dilemma, but as for now, I will happily avoid doctors at all costs! It is too bad one of them is on my support team, but that is God's humor at work! And I have never gone to see her in her office, so she doesn't seem to be a doctor.

3) Sickness

I will go to great extremes to hide illness. Always have, always will. I am the opposite of a hypochondriac. To admit illness for me is to show weakness. In my youth, my mom would take me straight to the hospital as instructed if she knew I was unwell. Yes, it was a research hospital and they were keen to see me in my elementary school years for studies, but it seemed to me the cycle of illness stopped when I quit being taken to the hospital. I didn't have to go lie in those beds where I was often tied down by tight sheets and not free to go to the playroom where I could hear other kids having fun.

2) Soggy Food Issues

I remember breakfasts in hospitals in my youth. I am confident I barfed many of them up! The toast was pre-buttered and usually cold. When you picked it up, it would fold over on itself. Yuck! For many years, I did make toast for breakfast: it would go in the toaster until dark brown and then straight into the freezer until it was hard and cold. Then I could add butter yet leave the toast crunchy. Why did so many food issues develop? I blamed it on soggy food, but it could have been other memories were triggered. I am not sure. Those may still come in time, but for now I have cravings for crunchy food. When I am stressed or sick, give me dry bread sticks please! I still can't eat sandwiches or burgers at a restaurant unless I trust they can provide the bread or bun toasted and dry with nothing on it. Crazy but that is me! I am better with foods now, but also very careful about what I will try. Therefore, the safest thing on a menu at a restaurant is chicken fingers and fries. That is getting very tiring!

1) Sexual Abuse Itself

All the symptoms above were just signs and somehow con-nected to the deepest pain: abuse. The memories came as isolated little pictures, like mini slide shows that never told an entire story start to finish. I had always felt this meant I was just crazy, but this is most common with serious issues of abuse.

Breakdown of the thalamus explains why trauma is primarily remembered not as a story, a narrative with a beginning, middle and end, but as isolated sensory imprints: images, sounds, and physical sensations that are accompanied by intense emotions, usually terror and helplessness.[41]

This inner place in my understanding tunnel is the one I share the least and need to feel I will be loved and accepted by the person or persons I share with. Otherwise, it is too big a risk and not worth it for my journey. If I feel my story will help them fine and good, but if my heart will be crumpled up and tossed in superficial conversation then it isn't worth it. Let's go for coffee I will say, rather than go deep in a passing moment.

Where is God in all the confusion? I wonder where the master creator was working in the layers of realization. All of us have made changes because of traumas even if we weren't aware of them.

Shame. What emotions shame brings to us. I made significant distinctions in my mind to work through these things. The shame is overwhelming, but it is not my sin. It was because of a crime done to me. I am not a bad person. I was a good person at the wrong place at the wrong time. The perpetrator is the bad person who sinned against me. As a result of his sin, I have carried shame in my mind as well as body tension for years. This is also why I was so rattled at the conference when I heard that the steps to healing would first include going and offering forgiveness to the perpetrator (see the "Introduction" again). That was not my first step and in fact can never be a step for healing for me as this doctor is dead. If I listened to that advice, I would be feeling as though I could not heal. Also, I need to be in touch with my own heart and do my internal work towards healing. Forgiving someone should happen once they first come to you and ask for forgiveness. Ideally it is a response we make once someone has come to apologize for the sin they have committed. (Forgiveness is dealt with in more detail in chapter 19.)

Shame
Horror
Pain
Distrust
Sorrow
Fear
Agony
Loneliness
Panic
Anxiety
Loss
Insecurity
Detached
Hatred
Self-hatred

Psalm 42

We all will face hardship, and we must draw near to God. The image in Psalm 42 of the deer panting for water reflects the longing of a parched soul. Nothing is more important than connecting with the water source when one is thirsting. Often the gentle stream seems hard to find during our troubles. Maybe our eyes are too full of water to see the stream or perhaps we feel it is too far away to reach. The psalmist was struggling as well, and we read that others ridiculed him for the place he was and asked where his God was. This was an example of bullying Old Testament style. Those around the writer felt God must have left him deserted because of the hardships. Some of you as readers may be told that you must have sinned and that you need to reconcile with God. Or you may be told you have an evil spirit that you must get rid of through an exorcism. Or maybe you need to do certain tasks for God to forgive you. Or possibly you are accused of not doing something you should have and that is why you are suffering. **Please know that God is gracious and loving; it is we humans who seem to have created hoops to jump through to be connected. God sent Jesus to break down barriers and bring the Holy Spirit to those professing faith.**

God loves YOU. You may feel as though you have been through the equivalent of the food processor and then the blender as Job had been. God has not punished you for being wrong. He has given humans free will, and we have managed to make quite a mess of things since Adam and Eve were in the garden of Eden. **The sufferings left from trauma are not your fault, and you did nothing to deserve these problems.** Unfortunately, there is also no magic wand for you to recover. You will need time and patience—something many are struggling with as well.

Going back to Psalm 42, let me share with you an excerpt from a devotion written by Pope John Paul II to a general audience dated Wednesday 16 January 2002:

> *But let us return to the image at the beginning of the Psalm; it would be pleasant to meditate upon it with the musical background of Gregorian chant or with the polyphonic masterpiece of Palestrina,* Sicut cervus. *In fact, the thirsting deer is the symbol of the praying person who tends with his whole being, body and soul, towards the Lord, who seems distant and yet very much needed: "My soul thirsts for God, for the living God" (Ps 42:3). In Hebrew, a single word,* nefesh, *means both "soul" and "throat". Therefore, we can say that the body and soul of the person praying are absorbed by the primary, spontaneous and substantial desire for God (cf. Ps 62:2). It is no accident that a long tradition describes prayer as a type of "breathing": it is as primeval, necessary and basic as life-giving breathing.*[42]

Breathing…Many counseling books emphasize the need to breathe and encourage yoga to become more in tune with one's body.

Our breathing does change with emotions: when we laugh, when we cry, and when we are preparing for something big. Being aware of your breath and using it to control tension is useful in the healing process.

Another phrase I would like to mention from this Psalm is "*tears have been my* food." Our bodies and minds respond differently from others under stress. Many eat when they are stressed as it provides a sense of comfort. Others find it hard to eat when they are under stress. Some of these changes might also be related to chemical changes from stress, so seeing a doctor is always a good idea (although I prefer not to see doctors as you know).

I have mentioned elsewhere in this book that you will be your most important therapist. You will need to be patient with yourself, and may need to provide your own pep talks when other positive comments grow silent. The psalmist does the same things, and it is a refrain that repeats in Psalms 42 and 43:

> *Why are you downcast, O my soul?*
> *Why so disturbed within me? Put your hope in God,*
> *for I will yet praise him, my Saviour and my God.*

This refrain puts the following picture in my imagination: the psalmist doing the equivalent of looking at himself in the mirror when he says why so downcast. He sees where he is, but he is not happy about it and knows that God is the solution to the predicament he is in. The same is for us. Give yourself a pep talk. You can use this scripture, or just chat to yourself, or find something to do for yourself to lift your spirits. Your broken inner child hiding from your trauma experience needs your care. Acknowledge the pain for sure, but remember to have hope: hope in God, hope in healing, and hope for the future. Long for this hope every day. Attempt to be future focused to alleviate some of the pain of past and present.

Prayer

Gracious God, help me. My heart is filled with shame. I am discouraged and I am tired. Hold me close to yourself. Teach me to keep my hand in yours as you guide me through this difficult journey. Help me to learn all the layers of pain I need to sort through, and teach me to accept and love myself. Give me strength on days when I am weak and feel too tired to continue my journey. Thank you for loving me on days I can't love myself. Thank you also that healing will come. I pray these things in the name of your dear Son who knew shame, sorrow, and loss. Amen.

Chapter End Projects

1) You are going to be your best therapist for sure. I am not saying in any way you shouldn't seek professional help in one or several forms, but you are with yourself more than anyone else. At two in the morning, there will be no one else to help you (well probably not). So why don't you try some role play. Put yourself in the role of counselor, and either use a mirror to talk to yourself or find a favorite teddy bear or doll that you may have around somewhere. I would not be able to look in a mirror to do this myself, so don't be surprised if you can't! So, what would you say to yourself right now if you knew you needed help? Try it. What would be helpful for you?

2) In this chapter, I evaluated layers that when peeled down ended at the sorrow and shame of sexual abuse. You will have different layers than I did as your situation is different. Every mental and emotional onion of sorts will be unique for each person. Spend some thoughtful time with this and you can either start with safest inward or greatest sorrow outward. Your choice for how you can best complete this.

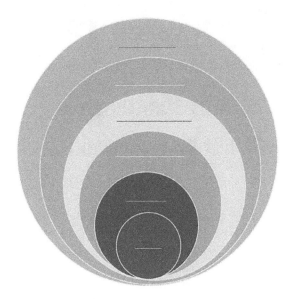

 Tips for caregivers

1) You also have layers of what you are comfortable with. Take some time to ponder your life. What are you afraid of or ashamed of? Why might this be? All humans struggle but we often lack self-awareness. It is easy to point out the problems and issues in others . . . much harder to do in ourselves at times.

2) Anything you can do to build the confidence of those around you is worth it. We are a community and we are stronger together as we are stronger individually.

Chapter 13

Molly Maintenance
What Do I Need to Do?

> Psalm 25:4–5
> *"Show me your ways, O Lord,*
> *teach me your paths;*
> *guide me in your truth and teach me,*
> *for you are my God my Savior,*
> *and my hope is in you all day long."*

What can we do to assist the healing process? How I would have loved a magic wand, or a magic pill, or the book that would solve my issues without me having to do anything. **Sometimes it isn't what we could do but what we should <u>not</u> do.** We have become so busy. We work more hours, run more errands, are attached to our phones for messages and e-mails, and we run for fast food as we don't have time to cook. I am guilty of those things as well.

As you become impatient for the magic wand to heal, you will always ask why? When? How? You will see they have also been repeated throughout the book, so you realize I too understand the longing for healing and for it to have happened yesterday.

Healing. If you have had major surgery, you know it is followed by weeks of being careful, of following the orders for post-surgery, for doing exactly as told by your physiotherapist if that is part of the process. We are told straight up it will be awhile. We don't realize of course until you awake from the anesthetic how you have been transported to a different reality for quite some time. So too it is with emotional healing. You are in surgery of sorts. You are solving a mystery and trying to extricate it for healing. But we don't have X-ray or ultrasound equipment for matters of the heart yet, so the work of the surgery team (you, your friends, and your counselors) involves diagnosis, then treatment, followed by healing and recovery. Recuperation time from this can be even longer than from surgery, or at least that has been my experience. Sorry for that news. At least I am honest!

Rather than pressure ourselves for the recovery and possibly miss some of the work that needs to be done, I recommend looking at what we should avoid doing that will help.

<u>What should we **not** do that might help us</u>:

A) We should not add more things to the to-do list to avoid the emotional work that needs to be done.

B) We should not become impatient with ourselves. The deeper the wound the longer the scar takes to heal.

C) We should not feel at any time this abuse done to us is our fault.

D) We should not hate ourselves for how long it seems to take on the journey.

E) We should not feel we must talk to people we don't feel safe with.

F) We should not make any drastic life changes during this time (also highly recommended until a grief process had been completed).

G) We should not feel guilty for investing in ourselves.

This list you have just read will provide some helpful tips to take care of you. Clear some room in your schedule, put your feet up, and be ready to do some intense learning and studying for this new role of taking care of you.

> <u>What?</u>
> A counselor who suggests I haven't been abused?
> What an excellent way to cause one to stuff forever!
> Who would ever make sexual abuse up?
> Maybe for a lawsuit? But I wouldn't do that.
> It didn't last for long though.
> Within weeks she was asking if I ever
> felt suicidal if I would please call.
> So similar to the chaos in my mind . . .
> Yes . . .
> No . . .
> Why . . .
> What to do?
> How to survive . . .

So we have looked at what we should not do, but that is just frustrating, right? We are still looking for the secret pill that changes all of life. Guess what? There still isn't one. In fact, taking a fast track can create more issues. You know yourself better than anyone ever will. A therapist knows you only by what you tell them, your friends know you by what they see in addition to what you say, but you and God know what goes through your mind. You know what triggers you and what helps you to calm down, you are the best chance you have for healing, so the choices you make are crucial.

The next chapter will give you some tips on what you can do, but this chapter encourages you to delete things from life that you can change. Now I am not saying to quit your job, sell your home, and give away your kids! We all have responsibilities. We do, however, often carry more things than we need. This will hinder your journey. If you are backpacking up a mountain, prepare your backpack for the trip and make sure it all fits. Then, take it all out and lay it on the floor and only allow yourself to pack half of the original contents back into the pack. This will make any real mountain climb easier. Same with any vacation as we tend to take more than we need and it becomes work to haul around and look after. Practice travelling lighter as that will make following the path that God has for you much easier!

Psalm 25

This Psalm was chosen as it starts with a request to be shown God's ways and accept His guidance. You have heard the expressions that God's ways are not our ways, but what are these ways then? Well, they will be different for every person on their own journey. We are not clones but unique people living our own journey.

Guidance from God is the theme of this Psalm, which is also an acrostic psalm as we had earlier in chapter 7. We don't know David's specific situation, but he speaks of enemies and the loneliness he feels. He asks for forgiveness for sins committed; this could have been something he did intentionally or something not done that should have been. Whatever the blemish, David felt badly. He was a friend of God and a great king yet David struggled. We should not be surprised when we also struggle. We need to evaluate whether we have a role that caused these hardships, but the most important is that we must rely on God.

In the complete Psalm, there are many tips to success in walking along God's path. See Figure 13:1

Figure 13:1 Tips to following God's direction
rather than our own from Psalm 25

What we need to be actively doing	Where do we read this in Psalm 25
Trusting God	Verse 1 (and much of the Psalm as well)
Waiting on God	Verses 3, 5, and 21
Being teachable	Verses 4,5, 8, 12
Being humble	Verse 9
Being obedient	Verse 10
Looking to God continually	Verse 15
Living uprightly	Verse 21

We nod our heads in an affirmative manner as these sound like rational expectations in relationship, but upon further investigation these projects are hard! See Figure 13:2.

Figure 13:2 Why Following God's Path Can Be Difficult

Trusting God	When trust has been betrayed by people, it can be difficult to trust in an unseen being.
Waiting on God	None of us want to wait. We are more impatient now as technology speeds everything.
Being teachable	It is hard to always be learning as we long to be done learning. Learning though keeps us alert and fresh in whatever jobs and life experiences we are engaged in. And, being teachable means not only learning, but changing based on learning.
Being humble	Humility is often easy for a victim of abuse as their confidence has been stolen. Shame tends to remind us that we are no good to start with, so humility is easier for us.
Being obedient	If we are truly going to walk in God's path, we need to do just that: put our shoes in the footprints He has left for each of us to follow. There may be times we don't want to follow that path as there are many distractions along the way that seem more engaging and fun.
Looking to God continually	If our eyes are God focused, we may miss seeing some other things. There is also an element of trust required to focus on God.
Living uprightly	We need to treat people better than we are treated. This is an excellent life motto to follow. We would do well to avoid dishonesty and communicate well in relationships.

You need to know that I struggled to find an easier path and a way out of the tunnel I was in. I trusted best I could with God's plan and His timing, but I was not the perfect child. I was impatient and tired of having to learn through this situation. It was like my regular life had been hijacked, and I begged for normalcy. Most people had no idea what was going on in my head and heart as thankfully I was working and working very hard. Work was, for me, an escape from the thoughts in my brain and the questions I was trying to answer. I read a book about workaholics that had a quiz in it. Turns out I am not a workaholic, but hard work did distract the black clouds by being involved in other things and having them go well. You may ask if I felt like a fake. Did I? Well, sometimes I felt like I had two personalities indeed but that was where it was so helpful for me to see my inner child as someone separate. Yes, I needed to learn of her fears and horrors, but the adult was taking care of the child. The adult of Molly went to work, bought groceries, cooked, cleaned (although never enough), and carried on like a true parent would. Molly was the child who was recently discovered and needed lots of care. When I could separate these thoughts and feelings, I was able to function. This may not be the best approach for everyone, but it did get me through, so I share that with you. I tried my best to follow the many tips for survival from Psalm 25, which I listed in Figure 13:2, but they are hard for all of us. Do not think of them as an all right or else you are wrong scenario. You set goals and try to improve. I have created a graph of three tough requirements to waiting for God's healing in Fig. 13:3. Some days are better than others for sure when you are struggling. But, it is this type of thinking you need. If you blow something, it is not the end of the world. You need to keep trying and be patient with yourself. When you can look at long-term trajectory, it will become clear that you are making progress. An analogy would be that when you are climbing up a mountain, it is often helpful to see how far you have come and not just how far you need to go yet!

Figure 13:3 – Hypothetical Grading of Molly's God Following in a Random Week

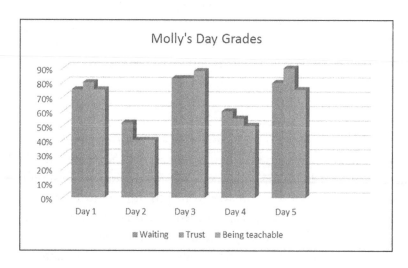

Molly's Day Grades

So, Fig. 13:3 shows something else. When I had good days, everything was easier, when I had bad days everything would slide. Expect that in yourself too. It is all about patience and the process. Healing from the trauma of abuse is not like flicking a switch. Remember that and be patient with yourself. **If you remember nothing else from this entire book, please remember you are valuable and worth all the effort it takes to drag yourself to a place of healing.** The air you breathe and the lungs you have for that are given to you by the master of the universe and the master physician of your heart. Just wait . . . wait . . . and keep breathing!

Now just a note as well that even if you are a teacher who loves to grade or an accountant who loves graphs, if you decide to mark yourself each day, don't get too obsessed. I never actually did this exercise in my process, but as I write this book I see where for many it could be helpful. This graph is a reminder that if you make a mistake in your day, you are not a zero. God will not toss you out with the evening garbage. We strive to be better as we are all human and all struggle with following God and being Christlike!

I used to reread my journals—or at least the ones I hadn't thrown out—to help see some growth and healing! If you have been journaling, this can be helpful for you as well

Prayer

Gracious God, here I am again. I am getting tired of struggling. Tired of climbing uphill with no end in sight. I need, as the psalmist wrote, to see Your path, and to be guided each step of the way. Give me hope as I try to learn to trust you more each day. Help me to see you in the small day-to-day challenges and give me renewed hope to carry on. Refresh me with Your Holy Spirit that I not be thirsty on the journey. Thank you, God, for holding my heart. Amen.

Chapter End Projects

1) How are you doing regarding the tips for recovery in Psalm 25? Make some comments below.

Trusting God	
Waiting on God	
Being teachable	
Being humble	
Being obedient	
Looking to God continually	
Living uprightly	

2) Once you have completed your thoughts in the task above, then make a list of ways you might make some improvements. Remember to accept yourself and be content do the best you can today and tomorrow.

Tips for caregivers

1) This would be another good time to remind the one you mentor that they have embarked on a difficult but important journey.
2) Pray for continued strength.

Chapter 14

Molly's Metamorphosis
When Will Deliverance Come?

> Psalm 6:4, 9
> *"Turn, O Lord, and deliver me;*
> *save me because of your unfailing love.*
>
> *The Lord has heard my cry for mercy;*
> *the Lord accepts my prayer.*

For real change to take place, the body needs to learn that the danger has passed and to live in the reality of the present.[43]

Metamorphosis is a transformation of sorts . . . an alteration. Altering clothing by a seamstress is so much easier than converting a way of thinking and responding to things. Staples, a retail store in home and office business products, has a little red button called an Easy button. You push it and it says, "That was easy," and I bought one, but it didn't help. Working on how your brain and heart respond to triggers and memories is not easy at all.

The approaches to healing will vary tremendously among victims. Many have tried the following:

- Hypnosis (I haven't but did ponder it for a few weeks)
- Counselling (I have)
- Journals to "speak their unspeakable" (I have)
- Attending groups of like sufferers (I did not, as I did not want to be in a public group)

- Classes such as karate to feel safe (Not me, are you kidding? I am not athletic!)
- Visiting the places they were abused with a counselor to try and desensitize (I did not, but my mom opened our family home to a lady and her therapist to re-experience her childhood trauma.)
- Massage to help them feel connected with their bodies (I enjoy massages but not sure if that has helped my recovery from trauma.)
- Prescriptions to assist the process. Remember though that these help you maintain and carry on but will often cover up the underlying issues that need to be addressed. (I have taken pills but very carefully under a doctor's care and nothing I would be addicted to such as sleeping pills.)
- Take time to themselves to "hold" their inner child. (I have taken time to care for Molly.)
- Attend rebirthing sessions or hug therapy sessions (I have not)
- Various types of therapy such as rapid eye therapy (I have not)
- Dramatization of their experience but changing the dynamic, in a sense stopping the event film and changing the outcome (I have not)
- Confronting the abuser (I did not have that chance)
- Taking their abusers to court (I did not)
- Involvement in drama, music, and art to find a way to express their feelings, or to create new ones (I have always found classical music therapeutic.)
- Reading about other people's situations and experiences are very helpful. (I have for sure.) This is a way to be part of a group of survivors without having to be a visible member of the group!
- There are other things too.

My best moments of feeling in touch and being able to recover from a trigger have been to light a candle, find some quiet space, and write. Not all things written are kept, but at least they have been externalized in some form. Not all find writing helpful, but pen in hand in a nice book is still more gratifying for me than doing a similar thing by computer!

> Eyes
> windows to the soul . . .
> For some the windows have black out blinds
> For some a drape to filter reality
> For some there is a fog of confusion visible.
>
> How can one change their eyes?
> To change how they view the world?
> Or how the world views them?

The most important element for metamorphosis, however, is time. If you do journal, stop and look back over time as that can allow you to better see the progress.

Be patient toward all that is unsolved in your heart and try to love the questions themselves . . . Live the questions now. Perhaps you will gradually, without noticing it, live along some distant day into the answer.[44] (Raine Maria Rilke)

How do we deal with triggers when they set us off? I have stated some triggers for me earlier in this book. Things like medical appointments, soggy food, and people who are dishonest.

What do I do for me when I have been triggered and my stress rises? I have mentioned a few earlier, but here is a short list of what usually works for me:

- Writing
- Burning candles in a peaceful environment
- Having a nice bath
- Reading scripture and/or praying

- Going for a car ride (once I evaluate I am safe to drive of course)
- Going outside and sitting with a nice view of a garden or a lake/river
- Listening to music
- Having a nice cup of tea or a quad latte
- Calling a friend even if I am too upset to talk

Think about things you can do to help you cope. You will of course face challenges in life as we all do. You will face fears again in life, so how do you take care of yourself? What can you do to protect yourself from situations that could trigger you?

The question at the start of this chapter is "When will deliverance come?" You may notice that I couldn't provide an answer for you! Don't be jealous as I couldn't even solve that for myself. I hung onto many little things hoping they might solve all the issues. I remember I was working on a very tricky puzzle, probably one thousand pieces, but I don't remember. I like puzzles as it is nice to see chaos turn into something lovely in the end. In a particular puzzle, there were too many of the same color left and I felt there was no hope. I had friends help me. I started to joke that when the puzzle was done in real life, it would be a sign that Molly's work was also done. Well, you are smart and know the end of the story. The puzzle on the table in my living area was completed. Every piece did have a home. That puzzle was solved and in much quicker time than it takes to solve any trauma issues. Oh well, it is okay to make a few games out of the process as it does at least keep you going, right? It also gave my friends a very tangible way to feel they were helping the process even if it was quirky!

Psalm 6:4, 9

Turn, O Lord, and deliver me. (v.4a)

Some translations say "turn," some use the word *return* as the opening to verse 4. This verse by the way follows verse 4, which echoes a similar theme for us of how long? The prayer that follows is a request for God to come back somehow. Why would God have His face away from the psalmist? And does God turn His face from us? Does He leave us at times only to return upon request? Or maybe it is us that has moved away from God? Or maybe we don't see Him because we do not cast our eyes His direction enough? God is omnipresent, which means He is always present. He doesn't wander off and leave us. He may not intervene when we think He should, but He is always there.

And how about the word *deliver* in that verse? Deliver can be rescue, set free, save, or release. These are all words we desire in our lives. We desire sleep when we are kept up at night with our minds whirling. We want to be set free from the memories that are triggered by various life experiences. We want to be released from the past and set free into the present. Can we beg God to turn to us when He is always there? No, but we are drawn closer to God when we realize that our deliverance comes through God alone.

Save me because of your unfailing love. (v.4b)

The psalmist in the second half of this verse highlights the key to life, and that is that God has unfailing love. **God is dependable.** We cannot trust in humans 100 percent as they will fail us and hurt us. But God loves us always even when we cannot feel that love. And it is because of that love that God will save us. How are we saved? We can be healed in mind, body, and spirit through God's work in our lives. This will be a metamorphosis for us, and it comes by God's care and love for us, not by something specific we do. We do, however, need to do all we can to care for ourselves as God cares for us.

For example, imagine someone diagnosed with type 2 diabetes later in their life. God may not heal them directly from this, but through medical science the tools are there to help that person between diet and insulin to care for themselves. The saving God has done this through the creative genius of medical science, and if we refuse the treatments suggested by a new way of living, we will suffer the consequences. So, we ask God to save and deliver us, but we have responsibility as well to take care of ourselves as best we can. Repeated throughout this book is the notion that you will be your best counselor. Know that God loves you, but you need to be active as well in the healing and transformation process. Because of God's unfailing love for you, you have a responsibility to love yourself.

The Lord has heard my cry for mercy; the Lord accepts my prayer. (v. 9)

God does love and hear the prayers of His people. Mercy is the key word in verse nine. He hears our prayers and acts not because of anything we have done, but because of our faith and our prayers. Grace. We receive because we believe. Knowing this truth brings us to our knees in thanksgiving. We are but a passing soul on this earth, but God, who loves us will walk with us through all. He will give us what we need to make it through.

Prayer

Lord, I wait to be delivered from these intense feelings of shame. My heart aches, and I need some relief that I may function in my real life. Teach me how to care for myself. Guide me to moments of rest so I can keep a balance between heart and mind. Help me to learn to acknowledge things that could be triggers and avoid them to keep my heart more at peace. Lead me to ask for help from others when I need it. Thank you for your patience. Amen.

Chapter End Projects

1) What are my most common triggers?

2) What helps me the most when I am stressed?

3) Stop for a few moments and pray through your list of triggers, asking God to help you with them. Remember the phrase in Psalm 6:9 that states God accepts your prayers.

4) Also ask yourself if there is anything from the approaches to healing list earlier in this chapter that you are open to trying as a new path to the inner heart.

 Tips for caregivers

1) What have you seen that has been a help?
2) Is there anything you can provide to make the path to deliverance a bit shorter?

Chapter 15

Molly Makeover
What Is the Purpose?

> <u>Psalm 18:2</u>
> *"The Lord is my rock, in whom I take refuge.*
> *He is my shield and the horn of my salvation, my stronghold."*

Is it better to hide one's head in the sand, to stuff one's heart and carry on, or is it better to walk through the road of painful memories to a point of healing? What are the advantages to following the journey? Some days the path is unbearable for reasons I cannot understand. Yet it would be nice to be free—free from shame, free from fear, free from hindrances to life that many of us develop to cope.

<u>What things have I noticed that relate to my abuse situations?</u>

*   I won't use a public washroom if anyone else is around. I have become a camel of sorts to accommodate this odd fear.
*   I never sleep the first night in a new place, whether it is in a hotel on my own with door bolted shut or in the apparent safety of a friend's home.
*   It was only recently in my healing process that I have been able to sleep without a light on. On my Christmas wish list at the age of fifty was a clock you could read in the dark. I never needed one before as I always had a light on! Wow! Our hearts that have been hurt significantly take a long

time to heal! Now I only need a light in places I feel less safe.

* I hate public change rooms in a pool facility. I crave the shelter of a curtained area and wonder how others can be so free.
* I hate doctor offices. I slip into a panic attack very easily.
* I also hate dentists! (Hmm . . . I guess who doesn't really?)
* I have many food issues. For instance, once the food is soggy, it creates an immediate barf reflex. Thankfully, I have been able to control this better over the years. However, the Yorkshire pudding on my plate never sees gravy!
* I have boundaries, and anyone too close or too "huggy" when I don't feel safe with them can set me off.
* I have learned to read people carefully. I am on high alert to read emotions and sense dishonesty.
* I try not to draw attention to myself by what I wear. Most of my clothes are a size too big, and that is perfect!
* Often, I am unable to detect the reason for a panic attack or flashback, but I am getting better at that and my own panic attacks have lessened considerably.
* I can see deep hurts in others easily. The more I travel this road of recovery, the more I see desperate people struggling more than I along the way.

I need to add, since I wrote about panic attacks, that items on the list above in and of themselves don't create a full panic attack. They increase stress levels only and can be significant barriers to a routine life. As I ponder, I realize most days I face a task or two that challenge my heart or mind, but the intensity has decreased with all of them thankfully. With my significant reading about abuse, I have discovered I am not alone. There are many people who struggle with some of these issues and then there are other triggers that I do not have that other survivors of abuse do. I am thankful, for example, that I have never been triggered by sense of smell. For many, the scent of a specific deodorant, soap, cigarette, or cologne can place them back in the midst of their abuse.

Fear seems to have a good memory, and our subconscious plays out the drama for us in the odd little fears we try to combat. They are not logical, and our minds can never make them logical. We need to try to understand yes, but we need to accept the struggles of the heart. We have to accept these feelings and memories as they come and accept them as the hurts of the past needing reconciliation and acceptance, not rejection. Each little step in this journey must be taken carefully as though walking with two curling slider shoes on an icy lake. Too large a step, some inattention, a push past one's comfort zone can send the fears of the past into a sense of panic. The small hurt child needs the confidence that his/her adult person will take care and not push her over the edge in frustration. We all need to be patient as we mend the heart broken in so many places. Patience, however, is most difficult!

Love of self is also essential for healing. Many abuse victims do not care for themselves in part because they feel broken and do not know what to do. I have been there. I have felt broken to the point of giving up—hours of crying, the desire to just quit, and wondering if there is any worth left in life. It is as though while so many others stroll through their lives, I am lugging a trunk holding the heart and body of my inner child as well as all the memories that I hope won't slip out at the wrong time. This is exhausting. I know. I have been to the point of giving up, and if I didn't have a network of friends, I may not be enjoying the life I have today. They could love me and care for me when I couldn't do it myself. I would ask, "Why do you like me?" and "When will I make it through?" or "When might you give up on me?" Thankfully, they were there for the long haul. I thank my creator God for His blessings of my support team.

I asked at the start of this chapter what the purpose is. Well, it could indeed be that I now have eyes to see others with broken hearts, I now can feel empathy and great sorrow that I can cry along with them. More will come about purpose later, but for now it has been helpful for me to know a few things:

1) While I have several odd quirks, my subconscious was actually protecting Molly from hurt by her grown up self, helping her avoid triggers and fears all while I did not understand.

2) Everything I learn about myself helps to unwrap a layer of a complicated and huge onion of sorts. Yes, that may bring some tears to my eyes, but there will be a core eventually if I press on in love and patience with myself and with Molly. Will it be worth it to be free? Yes of course!

3) That I have people that do indeed care about me is life giving to my heart. Being with them was like being hooked up to a battery recharger.

Is it worth the work? Back to the question earlier in this chapter: is it better to just hide your head in the sand? I think most of us prefer to avoid confrontation, which includes confronting our past issues. If we keep ourselves busy enough, maybe we won't feel the pain. It is often when we stop our regular routines, we are faced with the challenge of ourselves. Maybe this is why so many people never take their allotted vacation time?

Many victims spend so much time holding themselves together and keeping going that they never really

had a chance to process the trauma they experienced and the pain they suffered. (Barbara Engel)[45]

Engel goes on to list five consequences to stuffing your feelings and not dealing with the issues as they arise:

1) You end up not really knowing yourself.
2) You lose the good along with the bad.
3) Your emotions become distorted or displaced.
4) It's exhausting.
5) It damages your relationships.

The choice for staying on the recovery path is yours alone, and no friend or counselor can fully help your journey as they won't understand it as well as you. You will question what might be the purpose frequently, but you must have the strength to continue. It won't be easy even when you have come this far along, but don't stop now. That would be like being one course short of a bachelor's degree and deciding that is enough learning. **Keep going to the finish line!** Jump the hoop, get the piece of paper, and find peace in yourself. Keep climbing the mountain until you reach the top and see the quaint tea house just over the other side. Believe me, reaching the end is worth it and you are making progress even when you might see little change.

Once you are aware of triggers and can work through them, their negative affect on you will lessen. Make it a game of sorts to walk the line without going over the edge. Of course, you do not want to put your heart at risk, but you can work with someone else to strengthen managing skills.

We all like to try and set New Year's resolutions, and many of those are grandiose dreams about workouts, losing weight, quitting smoking, or saving money. In Fig. 15:1, we see that most fail at New Year's resolutions, but many commentators say we fail because our plans are too big. Change is always tough especially when they are changes of behavior.

Figure 15:1 New Year's Resolution Stats (based on a survey in October 2016)[46]

News Years Resolution Statistics	Data
Percent of Americans who **usually** make New Year's Resolutions	45 %
Percent of Americans who **infrequently** make New Year's Resolutions	17 %
Percent of Americans who **absolutely never** make New Year's Resolutions	38 %
Percent of people who are successful in achieving their resolution	**8 %**
Percent who have infrequent success	49 %
Percent who never succeed and fail on their resolution each year	24 %
People who explicitly make resolutions are 10 times more likely to attain their goals than people who don't explicitly make resolutions	

Check out those stats of how many are successful in achieving their goals: 8%. Wow. Why do we even try? The last box of this survey is hopeful in that if we don't set goals, we most likely will never achieve them. So, take some time and think through a trigger point in your life, just one and not all. Then try to create a successful plan for recovery. Imagine you are training a young child, or a new employee, and be patient with yourself.

Success consists of going from failure to failure without loss of enthusiasm[47] (Winston Churchill)

<u>Some examples of others who have struggled and made it</u>:

There are countless success stories from the Wright Brothers to Walt Disney and from Charles Darwin to Albert Einstein. I have chosen three women to feature in this chapter. I encourage you at this low point of your life to read about them and find some full biographies to read as well. This gives you the hope you can build on that humans can rise to a challenge and succeed even if society has analyzed their lives as insufficient.

1) Oprah Winfrey

Oprah was the daughter of a teenaged low-income mother, and their living conditions were rough. Her early story is one that includes sexual abuse starting at age nine. By the age of fourteen, she became pregnant, but her son died shortly after birth. Right after that loss, Oprah was sent to live with her father who helped her with schooling. She was later accepted on a full scholarship to Tennessee State University, majoring in communications. An early job also did not go well as she was fired by the producer because she seen as "unfit for television."

There is no such thing as failure. Failure is just life trying to move us in another direction.[48] (Oprah)

2) J.K. Rowling

She had written a few small chapters of her first book, but Rowling was jobless, recently divorced with a young child. She suffered from depression and lived off welfare. When she completed her Harry Potter script, **twelve** major publishing houses rejected her book. In 1997, a small publisher, Bloomsbury, took the risk and published one thousand books, with half going straight to libraries. She is now the most successful female author in Great Britain.

3) **Lucille Ball**

Lucille Ball had appeared in so many second-tier films at the start of her career that she became known as the Queen of B Movies. It wasn't until CBS picked her and her husband Desi Arnaz for a vaudeville act that her career launched as *I Love Lucy*. She has made generations laugh. Laughter is indeed a great medicine as it raises endorphin levels, which can be very helpful to physical health under periods of stress.

There could be another story very soon to add to my list:

4) _____ Your story . . . If you don't try you may never know what you are capable of . . .

_____

Psalm 18

Most Bible translations include an introductory comment to this Psalm. This was written by David when God delivered him from the hand of his enemies and more specifically Saul. The Psalm is repeated almost word for word in 2 Samuel 22, which was a thanksgiving song following a chapter of famine, and agreeing to allow enemies to be murdered to bring freedom. Many Psalms are quoted here and there but never in the direct context of being written as they are grouped alone into one book and not repeated. Psalm 18 is an exception, and this is helpful. We know David was king and was seeking a way to bring God's blessings upon the land. By the end of 2 Samuel, we do read that after David sang this song and built an altar to God, the famine was ceased. Most of earth's inhabitants know nothing of three years of famine. There have been difficult years for farmers on the prairies of Western Canada in the twentieth century but nothing that was close to three years without food.

The language of this Psalm seems very military like with shields and fortresses, but really it is a psalm that was praise to God from David as verse one starts with "I love you, O Lord." David's attitude for a successful project was not to take the glory himself but to give God all the praise. That is one excellent lesson for us. There is another too that comes in verse 19b, which reads, "He rescued me because he delighted in me." God did delight in King David. God also delights in us. He created us, He wants to see us succeed in life, and He walks with us.

In this chapter, I spoke of various behaviors my subconscious developed to feel safe. Yes, we all have some and they can be very quirky. BUT, the great news is that God loves us and accepts all those quirks. They do make us unique. The ones we want help being "rescued from," he can help us with that too. We need to praise God in advance in faith as David did.

What is the purpose of the lengthy makeover leading to healing from trauma? You may not know for years but being on the journey is most important. It could be long, it could be difficult, and you will hit road blocks. However, not to move forward would be a waste of an amazing life. As stated earlier, you are unique and gifted. Once you have been healed, you will have more depth and ability to help others, and you will be free to be more fully the person you have been created to be. Press on as it will be worth it! Even if that pressing on means waiting and being still.

The quieter you become the more you hear.[49] (Ram Dass)

The darkness
Afraid of the dark . . .
Fear
Need for control
Desire for security
Need to know.

50 years old and still afraid
Can't sleep in the dark
Can't sleep near anyone I don't trust.
Let me slip in, lights on, door locked.

Then there is the pattern of sleep.
Why do I wake up at 2am?
Why can I lie awake all night when completely tired?

The dark reminds me of
            loneliness
            sorrow
            boundary invasion.

Yet how strong is the sub-conscious and how does one heal?

How can we feel in control?
How can we face fear and make it through?
Why does the journey seem so impossible?
How does one obtain mental health in things they cannot
        reach, grasp, or even seem to comfort?

Prayer

All powerful and all-knowing God, help me to take refuge in your arms. Teach me to trust in you. Strengthen me and carry me when the road becomes hard to see. Guide me and give me hope for the future. Remind me that you love me and that I have a purpose in this life. Plant within my heart dreams for the future that I will better accomplish with these life lessons. Thank you, Lord. Amen.

Chapter End Projects

1) I shared in this chapter the stories of some important women who began their lives with struggles yet overcame them. What I would like you to do is write a short autobiography. I will give you an outline format below, so all you need to do is write your thoughts in those sections to get you started. Feel free to spend many hours on this project and be prepared to edit it as you grow over the years.

Autobiography format suggestions:
Section A

I) Birth facts. Born to_____ in _____. I have the following siblings, and we _____ (got along well/fought/stuck together/etc.) in our early years.

II) Early years: Talk about things you liked doing, liked eating, people you enjoyed seeing, favorite games and hobbies, and any special memories.

III) School life: You could talk about your school years highlighting important events, projects, and challenges.

IV) Career ponderings: What have you wanted to do?

V) Summary of struggles and abuse that have changed your focus and impacted your life.

VI) Where you are at in your journey now?

2) You have read the prayer about dreams and future. The past abuse has in a sense kidnapped your past and in a sense your present joy. You, however, can change the future by healing the past and better functioning and living in the present. **Remind yourself now that God does delight in you! God created you and loves you**. With the hope of healing in mind, let's take some time to imagine a new future for you. This step is hard and may sound crazy to

you, but I would like you to set goals and dream for this portion of the autobiography.

Section A of this chapter end project was historical nonfiction writing, and Section B is the completion of a fiction story, your dream story.

Section B

> Dream 1) How I make it through the journey. Who might help me, and how will I feel when I make it through to the end of this journey and on to a happier one.
> Dream 2) What new thing might I try doing that I have wanted to do?
> Dream 3) Everyone now speaks of bucket lists. We may think that is somewhat selfish, but for many of us who have experienced childhood traumas, we need to invest in ourselves a bit as we have lost time. What would you like to do? This could be a trip, helping others, learning how to paint, building a home, the options are yours.

This project of writing your story as real and hoped for is important. You also need to set goals and dream for the future. Setting goals now does not mean you can't adjust them later. The important thing is that without goals, you get nowhere! We have often used journeying concepts, let's do that again. You have planned a road trip to see several landmarks and attend several events over a two-week stretch of time. You plan ahead and have a map and a guide book. If your trips are anything like mine, you know that there needs to be flexibility. They may be a road detour for construction. You may get a flat tire and lose a few hours on a highway. You may find one place so exciting you decide to stay an extra day and give up something in the future. You may get called back to work early because someone has taken ill and you are in charge now. Flexibility is key to the future, just as being patient is key to healing the past. You may be tempted to try to structure your life to make up for lack of structure before, but there are too many factors for that in most people's lives. Having the plan for the road trip is important, but being willing to allow flexibility is key. There are many routes and many options to a successful future. In a few chapters (chapter 17), I will present thoughts about shifting into the future from the past, so this exercise is helpful to begin thinking along these lines!

Dream!
This is your life . . . enjoy it to the fullest
now and into the future.

Remember every day is a gift!

 Tips for caregivers

1) Ask if you can read some of their story? Or, there could be some journal pages they would like to share with you that they can't vocalize but would have you read. Then you can help them with their past story some.

2) You may be seeing gifts in the one you mentor. You may choose to share those things as the journey continues.

Chapter 16

Molly's Mirror
What Will I Become?

Excerpt from a Molly Journal October 2016

I have been a month working full time on my 'Molly Project.' I have been doing a mix of reading (on psychology, abuse, and the book of Psalms) as well as some writing scattered throughout the chapters. I was reading about another woman's journey through abuse when life ran me over with crisis and brought me back to a remembrance of the emotions and stress of my darkest days. My brain has been in memories of trauma, but my heart was stable. However, a dog becoming quite sick and forcing me to an emergency pet clinic with a poor diagnosis brought me to a place I haven't been for a few years: ...

> ... - Stress
> - Tears for hours at a time
> - A reminder of how lonely I truly was in my journey (no family, no friends who were available to be with me those few days...)

Two hours in a small diagnosis room, leaving my dog, having several phone calls from Dr. Melissa. Too much. An author I was reading about at the time spoke of "the fog" when she was overtaken by feelings from the past. (*Sorry I can't remember the author. I must have been in a slight fog as well!*) I too slipped into a familiar place of stress, loss of hope, and inability to complete minor projects. It seemed life wasn't worth living. I haven't felt like this for a few years. It was a handy reminder of the importance of writing this book. The feelings are so deep and so emotional. It is like popping out of an elevator into a different reality. My brain is logical but when the elevator opens to a floor, it will remind me of hidden hurtful feelings and shame the emotions can often return.

I think one benefit of abuse is the depth of emotion one feels. This of course is not always seen as positive, but at least we have emotions and do indeed feel. Many others seem out of touch with their hearts, but those who have hit bottom know how deep bottom can be and how far it is to come back up.

I have matured, which gives me hope. I know I will face struggle, but I also know the reason for the depth of feelings and why I can crater with situations that remind me of my past. Because I can recognize these symptoms and know why they arise, I can accept myself and know that I will be okay.

I am usually a project- and goal-based person. I can usually press on. But I was alone for essentially two days and unable to complete any projects with a dog who was sick. My heart was too sad. I was worried about the dog and felt there was no one I could even talk to because I was so emotional. I couldn't talk about it for the first while.

That reminded me of difficult issues—they too are often too deep to talk about. That depth creates the following, I think:

1. inability to put the vast amount of emotion into words,
2. the difficulty to tap into deep emotions without time and patience,
3. the need to be in the right "space" to share these feelings, and
4. the high level of trust needed in someone I would talk with.

Unpacking the ability to unpack by speech:

1   Inability to put the vast amount of emotion into words

Why does it seem that speech is impaired with strong emotions? I found it most interesting to read from a researcher that the area of the brain that blacks out during flashbacks and feelings of high emotion is the area of speech. It is a similar area that affects the stroke victim.[50] I have heard people use the expression "just spit it out" when talking to people whose thought is hampered with speech blocks. The left brain is our logical side, and the right the more artistic and emotional. Research has noted that when "images of past traumas activate, the right hemisphere of the brain (they) deactivate the left."[51]

2   The difficulty to tap into deep emotions without time and patience

I have always found it difficult to switch from what I will call real-life into Molly-life. I can't just enter that area of my heart without sufficient transition time. Writing this book, I have the same issues. I can't just write for fifteen minutes, do some other projects, and come back. I need quality time. I need long term focus. Could it be that I must climb down into the tunnel and sit with Molly? Or maybe entice her to come to the surface? Think about your usual day: how many times are you asked, "Hey, how are you?" You give an answer that is autopilot of "Good thanks" or something similar. Now if we sit and have coffee with that person, maybe in thirty minutes, we might start talking. Same in a counselor's office, I may have driven through a storm, witnessed an accident, seen some road rage, been unable to find parking, etc. I see the first many minutes as wasted in therapy by unpacking the heart to even find it!

The Russians and Ukrainians have amazing dolls, matryoshka dolls, that nest inside each other. Each look the same, but as you begin to unpack them, they become smaller and smaller. Molly in my life has put herself in the very smallest of those to protect herself from danger and to protect me from the pain. It takes a while to disassemble all the bits of Molly's adult to find Molly in the smallest doll. She is there, a bit scared, but beautiful and needing care. When she sees daylight, it will take her eyes awhile to adapt to an open space with light and care.

Figure 16:1: Ukrainian nesting dolls

3   The need to be in the right "space" to share these intense feelings

I remember meeting with a pastor friend of mine at a breakfast diner. It was a tough place to open my heart. I would have preferred a darkly lit familiar space holding a nice cup of hot chocolate (maybe even with some Bailey's for an added bit of courage), but we do not always get a chance to create the perfect space. I am aware of this in my own life. One of my friends often visited in the evening, and she knew it would take a while for me to chat, during which time we often sat, watched a candle burn, listened to classical music, and then she would make sure I had wine in my glass as that seemed to help. Now, I wouldn't suggest too much alcohol consumption for sure! I have mentioned Bailey's and wine in one paragraph, so I should state that alcohol serves both good and bad; a little relaxes the stress, but too much covers up the issues even further and could create an addiction, which is another whole other set of problems that you or I don't need.

4   The high level of trust needed in someone I would talk with

Thinking back to the image of the dolls, remember that your broken heart has been protected by layers of careful nesting on the part of your subconscious. Until you are well along in the process, it is too risky and too hard to share your heart. Granted, talking is part of the healing process, but be aware that your heart is like a newborn baby needing care and love more than an intellectual conversation with anyone. While knowing there are issues in your life and being willing to deal with them, there is never any rush when it comes to mental health recovery. Some initial first aid, yes most certainly, but the healing is slow. Your talking to others about the pain you have endured should also be slow. I was slow. Very slow. I thought too slow for many who knew me, but I needed time. All the sorrow locked away needed time to resolve, and I needed time to understand it and accept myself. You will begin to know what true friendship is when you pass a pained and abused heart to someone else. They can either say, "Yuck, what an awful heart," OR they can begin to help nurse the heart back to life again.

This chapter is subtitled "What Will I Become?" I wondered in the initial trauma if I would make it; was Molly's adult strong enough to carry Molly through the tough stuff? It has been helpful

to reexperience the depth of emotion that was triggered by being in a vet clinic, feeling alone to be the support person, feeling the pain of possible loss.

Back to the dog as I am sure you are wondering. I cancelled everything I had scheduled and I sat for two days with my dog and held him until my shoulder even hurt. I felt I helped hug him back to life. That and some drugs of course. He made an amazing recovery.

The Lord does indeed help those who call. I reflect on my holding a dog for two days, crying over him and reminding him that he is a great doggie friend. That is exactly what my calling was with Molly as well. I needed to hold her and remind her that she was and is amazing.

During many of these years, I have had a picture on my wall, given to me as a gift from one of my support team, as a reminder that God also holds Molly in his arms. The artist is David Bowman, and the title of his work is *My Child*. I have included here a photo of my print. Please see the end note for ordering information and other great art pieces available.[52]

Figure 16:2 *My Child* by David Bowman

Psalm 37

We looked at a portion of Psalm 37 back in chapter 7 enti-tled "Muted Molly" and noted it was the wisdom Psalm that was an acrostic. The overall message in that chapter was do not fret and wait patiently for God's perfect timing. The verses of Psalm 37 we feature in this chapter come later in the Psalm—and often much later in life for us. They come with the perspective of time and not during the chaos of life. Verse 1 of the Psalm is anxious, but by verse 40 there is calm. For Molly, there were many years between initial cry and a sense of acceptance and love.

The salvation of the righteous comes from the Lord. (v. 37:39a)

This salvation can be from short-term crisis and struggle, but also can refer to the ultimate salvation of our souls made through the sacrifice of Christ on our behalf. We are saved, and that comes from Jesus who we recognize as supreme Lord. If we have looked at freedom from struggle through drugs, retaliation, or any other num-ber of things, there is one source only. All types of saving come from our creator who provides true and lasting healing. Salvation brings wholeness, something we all long for.

He is their stronghold in time of trouble. (v. 37:39b)

Stronghold isn't a term used frequently, even the best glues in the world doesn't last forever. As a noun see the following definition in Figure 16:4

Stronghold: noun
1.
a well-fortified place; fortress.
2.
a place that serves as the center of a group, as of militants
or of persons holding a controversial viewpoint[53]

Figure 16:3 Dictionary.com definition of a stronghold

In our current world affairs, nothing seems to be well fortified. Terrorists have left us to feel that nowhere can be truly safe, may it be a shopping mall, an airplane, or at times even our homes as we have many alarm systems installed in private homes to avoid potential intrusion. God provides us a safe place, and for that we are safe in the long-term big scan picture. Yes, the details may be difficult, but we may rest our troubles in the fact that the one in charge of all things sees us.

The Lord helps them and delivers them. (v. 37:40)

The Lord does help us. At times, it may not be the way we would have chosen at first, but with hindsight one can see the present and the future so much better. In healing, we do not forget our past, but we can look upon it with confidence that there was a plan much larger than us. We wait for deliverance, and it will come. Others will try and help us too. Remember that as humans they may fail and disappoint us, but God will be consistent. We can trust in Him.

He delivers them from the wicked and saves them. (v. 37:40b)

Who are these wicked? Well, that of course is God's decision ultimately, but for those of us who have been abused, we know who has been wicked towards us. They may never be accountable for their actions in this lifetime, but God as Father, Son, and Holy Spirit is aware of all things. We can trust God. In fact, in doing that we also know that we are left to deal with our lives alone. Our perpetrators have their own personal battles to fight. We can leave them with God and know we will be saved.

Because they take refuge in him. (v. 37:40c)

We are saved when we take refuge in God. Refuge in him. Being "in" is more than just shaking hands with or acknowledging the presence of God. We are called to take refuge. God will not force Himself on us as our abusers once did. We take the action here by making a life choice to be friends and trust the Almighty. We take the first steps, and God follows through with more than we could ever hope or imagine. There may be a time of waiting, yes, but God is calling each of us to His side. Molly and your inner children are all called to take refuge in the fortress. They do not need to hide in the closet to be safe. You and God are called to a team project of protecting and strengthening your inner child.

Luther closes his Exposition of the Psalm with the words, "Oh, shame on our faithlessness, mistrust, and vile unbelief, that we do not believe such rich, powerful, consolatory, declarations of God, and take up so readily with little grounds of offence, whenever we but hear the wicked speeches of the ungodly. Help, O God, that we may once attain to right faith. Amen."[54]

Prayer

Gracious God, thank you that when we take refuge in you that you bring healing, comfort in safety, and salvation both now and eternally. Help us to stay "in" you and not wander. Give us eyes to see the larger picture. Thank you for saving us and rescuing us from evil. Deepen our faith that when we look in our internal mirror we see you at work in our lives. Let us see that through this journey we have faced that we have become better people: we feel, we care, we have depth, and we know what it is like to be rescued. Draw us closer to you throughout our lives. In the name of Jesus, Amen.

Chapter End Project

In this chapter I used the image of the nesting dolls as a visual for the work needed to unpack the heart and deal with the issues at one's depth. Below I have created a project for you to color. Maybe make a few copies first so you can be very creative. You can do the usual of identical dolls, but you can shake things up a bit too. Might I suggest you ponder your layers and create a new design for each. We all have a "public face" that we can show the world, then we might have a "face when I am with family," or "face with my best friend," or "face pondering trauma." There are many options to creating this project.

What I want you to notice is that the smallest doll I have here opens to a heart, a tiny beautiful heart. For me that heart is Molly. She hasn't grown much over time as she has been so sheltered with layers of protection, but there she is. Beautiful and worth more than all the others as the emotional heart of the operation. This heart runs her big person and all the layers in between.

Have fun and remember there is no right or wrong way to do this of course but millions of options. Create, ponder your layers, and also see some beauty and reason for each.

Tips for caregivers

1) You may not feel as though you have artistic skills, but try doing the nesting dolls project of what you see of the one for whom you give care. Often, we can be a benefit by sharing perspective from a distance.

2) Continue to pray for healing and restoration. God hears the prayers we speak.

Chapter 17

Maturing Molly
When Will the Joy Return?

> Psalm 51:7–12
> *"Cleanse me with hyssop, and I will be clean;*
> *wash me, and I will be whiter than snow.*
> *Let me hear joy and gladness;*
> *let the bones you have crushed rejoice.*
> *Hide your face from my sins*
> *and blot out all my iniquity.*
> **Create in me a pure heart, O God,**
> **and renew a steadfast spirit within me.**
> *Do not cast me from your presence*
> *or take your Holy Spirit from me.*
> *Restore to me the joy of your salvation*
> *and grant me a willing spirit, to sustain me."*

Psalm 51

Psalm 51 is one of the seven penitential Psalms or poems reflecting great sorrow for sins committed. There is a title to this Psalm, which in the NIV reads,

> **For the director of music. A psalm of David. When the prophet Nathan came to him after David had committed adultery with Bathsheba.** (Psalm title)

Oh dear . . . David was called out for his sin by a prophet. The story is found in 2 Samuel 11 and 12 and reads like a movie plot. I discussed his transgression back in chapter 1 so that you knew David was more than a little boy who killed Goliath with a small stone! A quick review: David commits adultery, Bathsheba gets pregnant, and then her husband is murdered to try and cover up the story. Hmm . . . David did not seem to show any regret until the prophet of God showed up and the story came out. David could have followed the same path and then murdered Nathan, but instead he recognized his sin and begged for forgiveness from God. God allowed the child born of adultery die, but David who was then married to Bathsheba had another son with her who was named Solomon. Solomon later became a great king as well as his father, David.

David cried before God for restoration for the sins he committed. The feelings he had of deep anguish had a specific story caused because of his own many sins. Yet the feelings of sorrow and depression easily match the heart of one who has been abused. I have created a chart of the feelings expressed between verses 7 and 12 and how we as sufferers of abuse can relate to these themes so easily (see Figure 17:1).

Figure 17:1

Similarities in feelings	Comparison between David and the heart of one abused
Need to be cleansed (51:7)	The abuser and the one abused feels "dirty" and in need of being washed. For the one who has been abused (Molly in my case), there is a feeling of being dirty from shame although the action was not her fault. David, the author of the Psalm, needed to be cleansed from the sin he committed.
Desire to hear joy and gladness (51:8a)	Sin and shame both bring a dark cloud of depression. For David, he would feel he doesn't deserve joy. Molly was so heartbroken; it was hard to experience positive feelings.

Bones feeling crushed (51:8b)	Mental anguish does have an impact on our bodies. We feel gut-wrenching pain. These feelings would be quite similar between King David and little girl Molly. (I have never felt bone crushing thankfully.)
Wanting to be hidden from God (51:9)	David was embarrassed at his wrongdoing and desired that God erase this memory. Molly, and her many equivalents who are reading this book, has been hiding from fear. She wants healing to come that she doesn't feel she needs to hide.
Desire for a pure heart (51:10a)	When your heart is broken, you crave a new heart, one that is healthy, happy, and working. God doesn't do heart transplants as are medically done now, but healing from sin and shame can create a pureness and renewal.
Renewal of spirit (51:10b)	Renewal of relationship with God is the cry of David, but should also be our cry. Molly also prayed for a renewal of mind. Much like a desired recovery from PTSD, the broken mind needs to be healed and renewed.
Restoration (51:12a)	For both David and Molly, there is a need to have joy restored. Restoration in relationships is key for the joy to return. They need to forgive themselves, be in relationship with God, and restore relationships they may have hurt in their journeys.
Strength to sustain (51:12b)	Ahh . . . the desire for the future. The desire to move from past and present into the future. This is a key theme in this chapter and is a key sign of healing. Many who are too depressed cannot carry on. They are overcome with guilt and sorrow and take their own lives. Pray for the strength to deal with the past. And then, continue to pray for that as this is a long process.

The pendulum

A pendulum is a weight suspended by a pivot of some kind that the weight may swing freely.

Of course, there is a resting spot, an "equilibrium position" of sorts.
When some kind of force is applied, the weight begins to swing.
It should swing from one side to the other.
Pendulums are affected by outside influences such as "air drag" and friction.
Galileo began to study the pendulum in 1602.
He was sparked in research by the swinging of a chandelier many years before.
Galileo obviously took time to ponder!
Swings . . . they are far more than a study in physics.
They can also reflect our minds and hearts.
How often can we truly say we are in an "equilibrium position?"
We would like to think we are completely stable—free from friction and tension,
free from the "drag" of life and people around us.
Yet we struggle to stay centered.
For the mind and heart have been off balance through crisis or tragedy.
I ponder with the pendulum the issue of past, present and future.
My past has been locked up (by what seems to be a huge lock)

by the subconscious trying to maintain a balance of sorts.
There are so many ways to relate this:
avoiding the swing to the past
trying to focus on the future (and when will the painful journey end)
being overwhelmed with the past one cannot experience the present
when the hidden fear and shame are settled, it seems to take so very little friction to swing into the past
for so many issues of the past are not of our doing, but the pain and loss is so significant we struggle to get our

pendulum in balance.
Many things can cause this pendulum to swing and many of them seem unknown
When?
How?   ...

> *... These are the puzzles of the heart that science seems unable to solve!*
> *When does healing come?*
> *How can one heal when they struggle to balance head and heart?*
> *Our minds can't seem to understand the workings of the heart. The mind tries, but fails and becomes as discouraged as the heart.*
> *The pendulum is so bogged down it can't even swing. It is caught, friction, tension . . . and obstacle.*
>
> *When can balance be obtained?*
> *How can I help that process?*
> *Where is God's healing hand in the midst of the physics of the heart and mind*
> *and of the past, present, and future?*

As my poem "The Pendulum" states, there are emotional swings of heart which below are in visual form. The pendulum takes us frequently from rational to emotional often without warning. We feel most stable when our mind is in control, but some stretches of time seems more like luxury than anything. It doesn't matter what our IQ is when it comes to matters of the heart. In fact, if anything, the higher our smarts level, the slower the process is because we interfere with the process of healing. We are more likely to stuff and ignore our hearts if we let our minds run the show, but we don't deal with the core issues and therefore never truly heal. I also know even as I write this book that as I spend more time with issues of the heart, I am far more emotional than usual: I cry during the news and not just during movies! Yet if I don't open my heart to the various emotions, I cannot heal from them.

Figure 17:2 reflects the challenge of the head and heart often being at different places, and we try desperately to gain balance between these two poles.

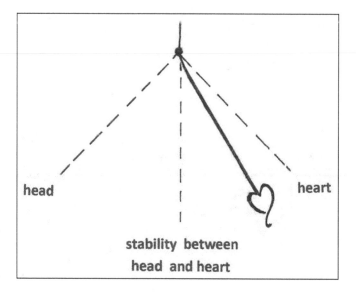

Fig 17:2, swing from head to heart

head

heart

stability between
head and heart

The other issue of course is that it is very difficult to live in the balance of the present when struggling with flashbacks, dreams, triggers, and so on. We are bogged by the weight of past issues, and while we want to sort them out, which requires living through them, they are a distraction. Being pulled into the past where we have so much hurt, sorrow, and shame distracts us from joys of the present and being able to look forward to things in the future.

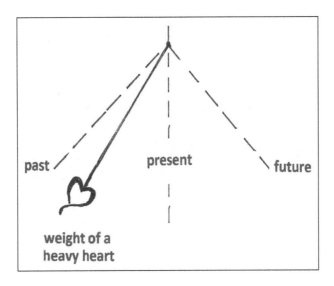

Fig 17:3, swing from past to present

past   present   future

weight of a
heavy heart

The journey of abuse has one thinking and feeling in the past and therefore struggling to cope with the present and the future. One's heart is pulling to the past and interfering with real life.

A sign of healing for me has come when I could these:

1) Look at the past and see that it has made me a better person as I can feel more deeply. When I accepted the past, realized it wasn't my fault, and was able to love myself, then I can release the pain of the past.

2) Live in the present in various situations and not have my heart carry me off by triggers to painful memories. This is very hard. Very seldom with a pendulum swing is the pendulum in the exact equilibrium position of balance and focus in present. Looking at the Figure 17:3, maybe 5 percent of the graph time could be considered present. That isn't very much of actual thought life. The goal of the healing process is to reduce the distance between swings with the graph looking more like the one in Figure 17:4.

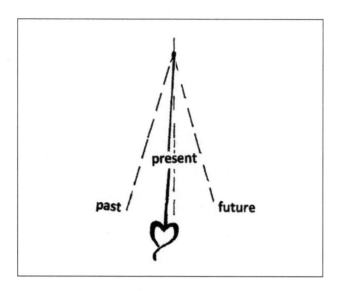

Fig 17:4, Less distance between
past, present, and future

With less swing, and therefore the past being not so deep or far away, we are always closer to the present. Trust me that with steady work to solve the past, the present will be more obtainable.

3) Long for future. When one is truly discouraged and depressed, they don't care about the future. They don't plan special events, they don't bother saving money for the future as they can't see hope, and so on. Remember when 911 happened? The earth seemed to quit rotating! People lost vision, and many seemed to think the world was about to end. The future requirement of dreaming was lost, and it took a while for people to regain any sense of hope. This was a collective response not just of those living in New York that day but of all those who watched the news. For abuse victims struggling with sleep loss, panic attacks, and stress, the future just seems like an extension of the suffering. We ask "how much longer" rather than "what good

will come of this" or "what can I look forward to because of this." Again, going back to Figure 17:4 when the swings have settled on the pendulum, the future is in closer focus as well, which is a sign of better emotional health.

> *It is only in the darkness that you can see the stars.*[55] (Martin Luther King Jr.)

Many years ago, I would guess about twenty, I received a card that I liked so much I asked for it to be framed so I could put it up on my wall. The sentiment is life giving to many of us who have struggled with not having a past they had wished for, but it is a good reminder that the future is ours to create. The quote is attributed to Tom Robbins, but I am not sure who did the art work for the card.

It is never too late to have a happy childhood. You, however, will be the parent that helps your inner child to be transformed. Be creative with this project and enjoy!

Prayer

Creator of all, create in me a new heart and restore in my life a healthier balance between past, present, and future. Teach me to accept the past, live today as a gift, and long for the future which holds healing and ultimately the joy of heaven. Allow me to experience joy again. Heal mind, body, and spirit for my restoration and for your glory to be revealed through me. Amen.

Chapter End Projects

This chapter encourages you to be able to see past, present, and future clearly in the muddle of processing past issues. The projects I suggest here are tools from my workbench only. You may have other ideas that would be helpful for you, so I suggest you try them as well.

The unexamined life is not worth living. (Socrates)[56]

1) Past

Make a list of things that trouble you from the past. Not just things done against you, but also things you have done that you are not happy about. If you can't think of any, I encourage you to keep thinking. We all make mistakes. We all sin and fall short of God's glory. Being aware of these things will make you a stronger person in the sense you will be more compassionate to others as well as yourself. Humility is a gift which will put you in better connection with people.

2) Present

Now make a conscious attempt to shake the past to work on the present list. Ask yourself what you are happy about, and then what you are not happy about. Ask yourself if there are any positive changes to make today easier that do not affect the future. (I am sure many of you would say quitting your job and starting life over would be nice, but that is for most of us unrealistic. Sorry.)

3) Future

Back to the dreaming ahead list, here are some suggestions:

- What can I do for others?
- How can I make the troubled journey of mine lighter for someone else?

- How can I invest in my own life?
- What would I like to accomplish in the next two years and five years?
- What little things can I do that are childish fun based on the concept of never being too old? Easy ideas: Order cotton candy? Go to a Disney movie? Get my face painted at the fair?

 Tips for caregivers

1) During reminders of trauma, the past takes over as a type of fog which affects the present. Helping with future planning will help to offset the past and provide increased hope. You can help by planning something in the future: a night out, a weekend away, a joint project, planting a garden, etc. We all need something to look forward to.

2) Without pushing or stressing those recovering, try helping them set goals for the future. They could be as simple as painting an impressionist picture of the journey to healing, or starting to journal. It is possible that a change of city or job may be the only way to be free from the abuser. How can you help with future plans to freedom?

3) In recovery tips, I listed having a happy childhood at a later age. Maybe you can be the one to go to a parade with the one you mentor and see the excitement of floats and bands. Or go do bumper cars or mini golf one evening just to reexperience some childhood fun.

Chapter 18

Molly Is Me
When Will I Be "Normal" Again?

> Psalm 33:20–22
>
> *"We wait in hope for the LORD;*
> *he is our help and our shield.*
> *In him our hearts rejoice,*
> *for we trust in his holy name.*
> *May your unfailing love be with us, LORD,*
> *even as we put our hope in you."*

Sharing the story of Molly and me has felt like a risk. Over time, as Molly has grown and strengthened to be an equal partner with me, it has been easier. Many who I shared Molly with panicked that I had somehow divided myself up, and this would not be healthy. I could not live as two different people. I agree, but I have seen that many who have been abused talk of holding their inner child or doing special things for them in their journey, so I took comfort with my approach to healing. For me, it saved me from feeling my entire life was falling apart. The adult was fine; she has coped and excelled through difficult times. However, I needed to deal with this one room in my heart that hid Molly. I needed to spend time getting to know Molly's pain, caring for her, being patient with her, accepting her, and most importantly loving her. It was easy to compartmentalize her for twenty years or so until I could heal. Maybe it was not fair, but it allowed me to carry on in life, to make a living, to help others. I did not intentionally stuff Molly in the trunk. I heard her cries for help, reached out toward her, and it was in reaching out to her that I felt as though I might have an emotional breakdown! The adult was secure and at a point she could help Molly, and that is when my life began to shake for the better. I still think of Molly, and she still cries a tear for her loss of childhood and fear, but I accept her sorrow. I have wrapped my mind and heart around her and can see that Molly and I are indeed becoming BFFs as they say in pop culture.

Some people suffer serious depression from which they are not able to carry on after sexual traumas. When flashbacks from past abuse begin to erupt into their hearts and minds, they are unable to find hope. I am thankful my mind could still find beauty in the usual bustle of everyday life. In my struggle, I feel fortunate that I have held full-time work, been able to press on, and been able to minister to others. While my inner depth was not shared with many during the intensity of the process, it is from that same pain and depth that I strive to help others. To have others avoid the pain, the long journey to wholeness, the feeling of being alone . . . that is what I wish to help others with.

As this chapter is called "Molly Is Me," you can guess that indeed I have come a long way to feel a sense of oneness, and the chaos of living in the present with success and the past with despair have reconciled as one. Between Molly and myself, I feel stronger, and I have renewed energy and a strengthened passion to complete this book. I had found it very difficult to write many times over the last seven years, but as time passes and healing comes, I have a renewed energy to complete the task and press on. I am less concerned about the risk of disclosing my past and more concerned about writing something that can provide healing to others; this is proof to me that I can be "normal" again. There is healing, but only as you walk through the journey with patience.

> *Feelings*
>
> *Let them come*
> 　　　　*Let them flow . . .*
> *They have value*
> 　　　　*They have meaning!*
>
> *I too have value*
> 　　　　*and I have meaning…*
>
> *How long until that moves from head to heart?*
> *Why is the distance between head and heart so far?*
> *Is there hope for re-unification?*
>
> *The Berlin wall did come down!*
> *Maybe there is hope yet!*
> *One can pray for hope,*
> *One can pray that feelings are healed, understood, and accepted*
> *by the mind.*
> *Feelings . . . listen to them*
> 　　　　　*. . . invest in them*
> *They will bring restoration!!*

Psalm 33: 20 uses the phrase "we wait." I have chosen it for a few reasons: First off, it is Molly and me that have waited. She remained silent for years in wait. Then it was Molly's adult who waited for healing for years. Together we waited to heal on this journey we have walked together. The second reason I chose this scripture is that I know many like me who also wait for healing from trauma. They have called out to God or their gods in anger and impatience much as I have done. We all must wait.

My heart resonated with this scripture as I have waited in hope and placed that hope in God who loves me more dearly than I could know in this life. I have been able to worship God through these many years as I have maintained a strong faith. Even when I felt unable to attend church, I knew God loved me. I had seen him do miracles to give me life initially and then bring me back with life after sickness. Knowing He created all and knows all, I could trust that He would see me through.

Throughout history God has not disappointed, but often His people needed a long timeline to see God at work. For forty years God's people wandered in the desert. It would not have taken them forty years to travel the distance from the area of the Nile Delta to the land of Jericho, so they spent quite a bit of time wandering in circles. To continue wandering this way must have been a frustration for those who recognized signs of repeated geography! The issue there wasn't the destination clearly, but it was an issue of the correct timing. In the fullness of God's time they arrived after years of waiting and wandering.

That was forty years, but for seventy years many of God's people were in exile after being taken captive by the Babylonians. The prophet Jeremiah had stated the exile would be seventy years, but as historians have done their work there is much confusion over historical reality. Whether it was seventy years or a shorter length, the point to note is the vast number of generations! Many people would have been born, lived a full life, and died without seeing the promises of God fulfilled. A lifetime to wait with no resolution.

Waiting to never see fulfillment was true also of the early New Testament churches. They were told that Jesus was coming back soon. Hmm . . . we have waited two thousand years. These early Christians never saw the return of Christ, which I am sure they anticipated to be in their lifetimes.

The message we can take from these few examples is that **all is made perfect in God's timing.** Our trust in God must also include the trust in God's sense of the perfect time. We may never know the reason for what we see as excessive waiting. We are only called to wait and be still. So we wait.

You are in process in your healing journeys in life, and there could be many: sickness, death of loved ones, maybe a painful divorce, accident of a child, and maybe the trauma of abuse, etc. We all wait, and we need to continue to hope in God and His love for us. He alone knows the big picture, and we see so little. Trust in God and trust in the journey.

Psalm 33:20–22

The entire Psalm promotes reasons to hope as God is in charge over this fallen world and the people living in it.

> *Psalm 33 is a hymn of praise to God that celebrates God's righteous character, creative power, and sovereignty. These are all God's qualities that make Him the only reliable foundation for hope and trust. With this Psalm, the psalmist sets the tone of worship and reverence for the people of God, and we would do well to note that in the face of changing and challenging times, whether as a nation, as a church, or as individuals who are facing our own transitions of life, that God is where our hope lies. Our praise must reflect our reverence for God, our dependence upon God, and our hope in God."* (Lynn Malone)[57]

Transition is key wording in the sermon excerpt quoted above. We all have transitions in life. If we aren't evolving in some way, we are dying. Our body's cells rejuvenate year over year, our minds continue to learn, and our hearts mature through change and struggle. While we change continually, God's care for His people and His overall character does not. Verse 22 speaks of God's love that remains unfailing.

People will fail us in life. We are all human and are born into a world of sin. While we make mistakes, God does not fail us. We do best not to point fingers as those who fail but rather to give God the glory for the work He does in our world and in our lives. **Through God we have hope**. In fact, only through Him can we have hope. I have always been amazed at how the atheist can press on. There is no one bigger than they are to help them during struggle or loss. They may look at my book and suggest God is only a crutch in my mind, but I have seen God at work in ways that are unexplainable otherwise. So, because of what I have seen and experienced I hope and trust in God. I know God loves me, and even delights in what I do that brings peace and comfort through these times of transition.

This is the hope we all need—that God loves us. *Hope* is used twice in the span of three verses in this Psalm. Highlight that word in your heart. Hope dreams for the future. Hope sees positive in all situations. Romans 15:13 holds a great benediction of sorts for all people: "May the God of hope fill you with all joy and peace as you trust him, so that you may overflow with hope by the power of the Holy Spirit." Our hope comes from God, and through the Holy Spirit it can overflow in our lives. Wait upon God and trust Him. You will have great hope through the work of God.

So back to the question of the chapter of when will I be normal again? The philosopher would begin with the question of what is **normal**? A counselor might say normal **again**, when were you normal? I wonder when my heart becomes more peaceful and accepts the past, what the "new normal" will be. The state of normal will change for you as it has for me. The pain I have worked through has shifted my thinking and changed my focus to something new. I have been in transition, and through that I have changed. It has been good change, and it will be for you too if you accept yourself, wait patiently, and worship God in the transition.

If I were not to change I would be stagnant. I would much rather see the water in body, mind, and soul be refreshed and renewed than sit rotting as a swamp. Not good especially since I am not a fan of mosquitos! My concept of normal has changed, and that is good.

At this point, I bring in an illustration used in the Bible that speaks of radical transformation and not just a slight transition. God spoke to Jeremiah, as noted in Jeremiah 18:1–4, and said, "Go to the potter's house." So the prophet Jeremiah followed God's request. There he saw a potter with a pot on a wheel. When the clay took a wrong shape because of the potter's hands, he started again to make the pot more perfect. God later says he does the same with His people. The book of Isaiah holds a similar truth: "O Lord, you are the Father. We are the clay, you are the potter" (Isaiah 64:8a).

If we believe in God and trust in Him, we must also trust that He is creating us into something beautiful. And, if we are being created we are not normal or usual but vibrant and growing. If you are on the right track in life, I suggest you NOT seek to be normal, but be content with the process of being shaped into what God has for you.

I am reminded of the famous hymn "Have Thine Own Way, Lord" written by Adelaide Pollard in 1902. A negative experience inspired this poem. Adelaide had been hoping to raise funds for mission work in Africa. There was not enough raised, and she was discouraged. She went to a church meeting then overhead an older woman saying, "It really doesn't matter what you do with us, Lord, just have your own way with our lives." Pollard was so moved she went home and wrote all four verses for the poem before she went to bed. In 1907, George C. Stebbins wrote the music for this hymn, and it was published in its first hymnal that same year. The message of the poem is powerful, and I include it here. If you sing go for it, otherwise reread it over and over. Memorize the text and may God's spirit fill you to overflowing as you do.

Have Thine Own Way, Lord[58]
Adelaide Pollard (1862–1934)
Have Thine own way, Lord! Have Thine own way!
Thou art the Potter, I am the clay.
Mold me and make me after Thy will,
While I am waiting yielded and still.
Have Thine own way, Lord! Have Thine own way!
Search me and try me, Master, today!
Whiter than snow, Lord, wash me just now,
As in Thy presence humbly I bow.
Have Thine own way, Lord! Have Thine own way!
Wounded and weary, help me, I pray!
Power, all power, surely is Thine!
Touch me and heal me, Saviour divine!

Have Thine own way, Lord! Have Thine own way!
Hold o'er my being absolute sway!
Fill with Thy Spirit till all shall see
Christ only, always, living in me!

Thankfully, people have written about the inspirations they have received. I am sure this poem and song has been an encouragement to many people.

When we trust God as the master creator, we have hope that He will transform our lives into something of beauty, but this can take some time! *(What, I mentioned this before?)* While you wait, pray the words of this hymn over while God does His transforming work in your heart and mine.

Prayer

Creative God, I thank you for the work you have done in the world. For the many colors, the many plants, trees, animals, for mountains and valleys, for rivers and oceans. I thank you for the beauty I see everywhere. You are a master creator. Lord, help me to see the beauty in my own life through all of this transition. I have been on a journey, and you have walked it with me. For that I am thankful. Thanks for loving me and caring for me in the dark days as well as the colorful days. I do trust your work in my life, and I also say "have thine own way" in my life. Refresh my body, mind, and spirit that I may better reflect You and that I may serve You. Amen.

Chapter End Projects

1) What can you do to put your hope in God? What do you need to let go of so that you can hold onto hope in God alone? You may need to make some personal changes for healing. What could these be?

2) What do you know you need to change as part of this process?

 Tips for caregivers

1) How have you seen change and growth in people you care for? Take some time to ponder and then let them know with a short e-mail or card. I find it has been most helpful to have something tangible to see or feel and reread. Person-to-person conversation is great, but it is good to have something to remember these thoughts with. Molly's adult kept cards and often even the envelopes the cards came in for strength and encouragement. These can serve as a lifeline when you may not be present to help.

Chapter 19

Magnificent Molly
How May I Achieve Wholeness?

Psalm 31

Psalm 31 gave me great encouragement as it did for Jesus and Old Testament writers who quoted from this poem.

> *This psalm impressed itself on more than one biblical character deeply enough to come to mind at moments of extreme crisis. Jonah's prayer draws upon it (6), Jeremiah was haunted by a phrase from verse 13; verse 5 gave words to Jesus for His last utterance on the cross. And in old age the writer of Psalm 71, possibly David himself, opened his prayer with the substance of verses 1-3. It illustrated the role of the Psalms in meeting a great variety of human needs beyond the bounds of formal worship, and the original experiences of the authors.*[59] (Derek Kidner)

The entire Psalm 31 could be summarized in one word as distress. It, like many others, varies from worship and thanks to God on one side of the pendulum to prayer for help and release from stress on the other. Much like our lives! It is encouraging that Jesus quotes from scripture as it adds relevance to the Old Testament readings. He was mindful of the writings of the prophets, knew all about Jewish culture, the celebration of festivals, etc. Jesus respected God's word and the traditions of faith.

The psalmist never says that God will not send danger, or that we are somehow protected from evil if we go to church on a Sunday morning. No. The psalmist realizes there are dark days and difficulties for all of us. We are encouraged and instructed in the last verse of Psalm 31 that through faith and hope in God we can have the strength and confidence to make it through.

How can we "take heart?" Is that a sense of courage? David has experienced the down and dark, and it is because of that he can write, "Be strong and take heart." David has seen God work in his life and knows that faith can surmount many obstacles. I can echo these words from my life experience as well. When there is nothing to sustain your hope, turn to God. He will strengthen you.

Jesus came to this world accepting the past and moving forward along with it. That is the theme I choose for this chapter. **We need to accept the past and not reject it. If we delete the files from our person, we also delete an important part of ourselves.** Jesus did not throw out His Jewish heritage but strove to fulfill the promises within. We too need to embrace our pain and sorrow as an important part of who we are. For myself, I needed to respect Molly. She had held memories from me for years that allowed me to grow and develop until I was ready for them. She in fact has helped me more than I realized, so I cannot reject her. She came forward with pain, shame, and fear. Granted it was a shock to me and too overwhelming at times, but I do need to see Molly as magnificent! Because of the work we have done together, these last many years of journaling, counseling, pondering (and, might I add, lots of crying), we have made it. We made it without suicide attempts when the feelings of shame were too heavy. We made it without losing respect for the body, as many who have been abused work on the street. We have made it through with no addictions to cover the pain and hurt. For all these things, I thank God for His care and timing. And I thank Molly. That poor young girl alone in my heart just waiting to escape and yell for help. She waited until I had regained physical health, until I had made a strong faith commitment, and until I had completed my years of schooling and had settled into a job. Wow! My story is not unique—many have an inner child waiting to be accepted.

Accept your past, present, and future. If you have read the book until now, you show great interest in conditions of the heart and a desire to help either yourself or someone you know. Congratulations! You may not like everything you do sometimes but that does not change the fact you need to love yourself past, present, and future. When I ponder those thoughts, the famous book by Charles Dickens *The Christmas Carol* comes to mind. If there was a ghost to take me through past, present, and future, how would that change my life for the better? That is a question to ponder at a beach with a nice cool beverage and a journaling book. We should all do it.

> ***Learn from yesterday, live for today, hope for tomorrow.***
> ***The important thing is not to stop questioning.*** (Albert Einstein)[60]

Not only do we need to accept ourselves, but we also need to be at peace with the fact that God loves us past, present, and future. That is indeed the good news of the New Testament. There is nothing I could ever do to earn the gift I already have. We do, however, need to live in the light of that truth. That will shape who we are and what we do in our futures.

Accepting ourselves and our situation brings up another term that is part of the healing process, which brings us to wholeness. That is the word *forgiveness*.

Forgiveness

"Love your enemies." Hmm . . . this is a difficult message for those who have been hurt deeply by others whether through various forms of abuse, divorce, murder, bullying, and so on. In the book of Luke, this instruction from Jesus follows directly after the Beatitudes, which is the portion of scripture that turns regular thinking on its head to saying things like you are blessed when you mourn. This is radical thinking to most of us as we would prefer to assume we are blessed when life seems to be going well. Jesus then goes on to say the following:

But I tell you who hear me: Love your enemies, do good to those who hate you, bless those who curse you, pray for those who mistreat you. If someone strikes you on the cheek, turn to him the other also. If someone takes your cloaks, do not stop him from taking your tunic. Give to everyone who asks you, and if anyone takes what belongs to you, do not demand it back. Do to others as you would have them do to you . . . Be merciful just as your Father is merciful." (Luke 6:27–31, 36)

Turn the other cheek . . . hmm. We need some boundaries here to protect ourselves. And what do we do with the call to forgiveness? Those of us who grew up in a Christian Church have spoken the Lord's Prayer numerous times. There was a time in Canada when it was even recited in public schools, but those days have passed as we strive to be more multicultural and respect other faith practices. We have said the Lord's Prayer so many times, we don't even think about the words. Read with new eyes to the soul the following:

Forgive us our trespasses as we forgive those who trespass against us. (Matthew 6:12)

The word *trespass* appears differently in other translations as *debts* or *sins*. What do these words mean? In our minds, debts are much different than sins. We could think either that we are doing the easiest of agreeing to pay back a bank loan so that God forgives us, or a more difficult thing in forgiving others who have hurt us so that God forgives us. Feel free to check various online dictionaries and various scripture translation to see the varieties. There are many possible meanings, and therefore I suggest there could also be many approaches to how to forgive for these transgressions.

We can't begin to understand God's grace, but we need to accept it. If we realize how fortunate we are to have a loving creator who walks with us and guides us through all various paths and struggles, it is easier to look upon others with mercy. That is the reminder in Luke 6:36 about being merciful to others because we have received God's mercy. God indeed walks with all of us, whether saint or sinner.

—m—

Before I move on, I want to stop and remind you that when others have hurt you, you do not need to feel you must approach them or speak forgiveness to them. If you can forgive them in your heart, that is difficult enough and speaking to them is not a requirement for your healing. I echo the words of Allender who said the following:

> **Simply telling an abused person to love his or her abuser is unhelpful, even if love is an essential component of the change process.**[61] (Allender)

Forgiveness sounds easy but is very difficult. However, the act of forgiving someone else, even partially in our minds, does release the burden on our backs. Letting go of our anger frees us. If we retain the anger, we damage ourselves:

> **Anger: an acid that can do more harm to the vessel in which it is stored than to anything on which it is poured.**(Anonymous)[62]

We may not have the opportunity to forgive someone else for the wrongs they did to us as the opportunity may not exist, and it also may not be the correct route to take. If we can reduce our anger in some level of forgiveness and acceptance of the sins of all mankind, we help ourselves. We can forgive a perpetrator at least in part because we are all equally human, all make mistakes, and in God's sight are all sons and daughters. This part of the healing journey only truly comes after years and years of healing and may not be attainable for we humans. I think of the image of leaving a prayer concern at the foot of the cross and then going and picking it up again because we are used to the heaviness and it becomes comfortable. So it is with forgiveness—we may need to work on it in our own hearts for quite some time. **Do not pressure yourself to forgive, and do not feel you even need to approach the person who has hurt you**.

In a perfect world, those who have hurt you would come to you and apologize for their actions that have had life-changing implications to you and then you could say you have worked it through, had years of counselling, have had many life issues but are thankful they have come and you will work at forgiveness. I say this because true forgiveness is a very high calling. We live in a time when saying sorry seems to admit weakness that could more easily encourage lawsuit action, so apologizing is very rare in the situations where it is most needed. This increases friction and destroys communication between people.

Concerning this discussion of needing to forgive at some level, let me give you an example from my own life. I was in seminary taking a master of divinity program. My parents invited me for dinner, and I invited along a fellow student as her home was too far away for a visit on a thanksgiving weekend. I can't remember the situation that started the crisis, but I remember the fallout for sure. Dad was carving the turkey in the kitchen, had a temper tantrum, and threw the carving knife at me. I was in the dining area at the time. There was no physical damage to either the knife or myself, but the shock that reverberated through the rooms was a level 9 on the Richter scale. The evening was ruined, and we coped through in part because of a delicious meal. It is difficult to forgive a parent when they have failed in love and set a poor example of anger management. I never went to my father and said, "Dad, I forgive you for hurting me," as that would have caused another situation for sure. He could not see his mistakes, and I would have taken further risk to in a sense appear "mightier than thou" by forgiving him when he never could apologize for his mistakes or even identify them. That is why I can say from personal experiences that forgiveness is hard. I needed to forgive him in my mind best I could but not verbalize that to him or that would have been confrontational and set our relationship further apart. I feel the proof of my healing in my relationship with my dad came as I looked after him for a few years before he died. When he screamed words that would be censored while I drove him to appointments or dropped him off at the care home, I continued to help him. I did care for him, but my heart was more distant than when I cared for my mom in her last years prior. I was keenly aware of the difference, but I could look at Dad as a creation of God's who needed help. The detachment was there to protect my heart, but I could help him. That is what I see as "turning the other cheek." I was hurt but still able to care because I had thought it through, knew there was a bigger picture, and I knew my heart was in a good place. I had come to a place of forgiveness and was reaping the reward of freedom as I served. I will say, however, that the relief that washed over me when my dad died was a blessing!

With forgiveness, there may never be restoration of former relationship but there can be a sense of resolution. You need to take care of yourself first and then decide in your strength what else could be done. I recommend you get the help of your support network as they know you possibly better than you know yourself and they can give you guidance. I did appreciate the following statement made by Bass and Davis in their book:

(A good counselor will never) push you to reconcile with or forgive the abuser.[63]

That is a relief to me in many ways and I am sure to others as well! There should be no pressure on the innocent child who was abused to forgive the adult. Some may, but I do not feel it is an essential step that must be completed to achieve healing.

Much the same as a scar is visual evidence of injury, we all carry internal scars from disappointments in life. We may never be able to rid ourselves of the scars as they are a reminder of pain, but there will be a time when they no longer hurt and you don't even think of them.

So, as stated by the psalmist, be strong and take courage. Facing the idea of forgiveness is difficult and not a truly easy step. I have, after much reading and thought, prepared a chart of what I see as levels of forgiveness. This is to remind all of us that it is not black-or-white choice but many stages, all of which can be helpful. See Fig 19:1.

Figure 19:1 Common Levels in the Long Process of Forgiveness

	Stages
1	Accept your pain and suffering
2	Accept that God allowed this to happen
3	Know that God is with you
4	Be patient with yourself as you process the pain
5	Love yourself as you are
6	In your heart, release the anger against the perpetrator
7	In your mind, forgive him/her
Possible 8	Meet with the perpetrator and forgive them so they could apologize to you if they are able and they could begin their own work

You may find that your levels in the process come in a different order than I have listed. For example, maybe the perpetrator comes to you to seek forgiveness long before you have even started to identify the pain in your heart is from a situation of abuse. That might be the first trigger to start your memories as real experiences and the acceptance of flashbacks being real and not crazy dreams from a crazy life. That being the case, you might be able to forgive rather superficially that very day until you become in touch with the wave of pent-up feelings. Then your journey will begin. Because we are all different and our lives and situations are different, we will all experience this journey differently. There is no right or wrong way, but the best way for you at the time.

In the chart above (Fig 19:1), I listed a possible eighth stage. I have shared tips throughout this book on how I have made it through. I never completed stage eight. About the time, I had put things together and pulled a name out of my memory the physician who had been responsible for my abuse had died. I would have been in no way able to meet my perpetrator as he died by the time my memories surfaced. I ask myself now if I had the chance, would I? Being this is a hypothetical question for me, I am sure that makes it easier to answer. I have also sat on this question for quite some time. Also, you need to know I have rewritten these few pages about forgiveness more than any other part of the book. Once again, I say forgiveness is hard! I related in the introduction about being told I haven't healed because I haven't forgiven the perpetrator. That rattled my core and built a sense of rage in me I will never forget. I had so many other things to do before I could ever get there. I feel only someone who has struggled through abuse could ever understand that feeling. Going to this doctor and forgiving him before he would even consider admitting the sin (to avoid law suits), or apologize, or even respond to my comments would have been a challenge.

Back to the question, would I approach by abuser now if I had the chance? If I could live a virtual version of *The Christmas Carol* in my own life and relive the time, what would I do?[64] I think I could at least initiate a conversation and be level-headed. I wouldn't do it at this stage out of spite, or to make him feel guilt. I can't help but think the doctor's heart would ache if he saw the lasting damage and pain. My former pediatrician was given this young child to heal from horrible post-encephalitis headaches and her heart was broken as well. And this for research? Or for selfish desire or a power trip? How could this not rear up in his mind? I have wondered how this affected his life, his family, or the lives of the interns that watched and the nurses that must have known this was criminal.

The fact that I could forgive my pediatrician at some level now does show my process is done. But it has been about twenty years of little steps. Twenty years of walking up to the summit of the mountain. Was it worth it? Some days I wonder, but the freedom from baggage is a relief. The backpack I carried has been getting lighter all the time, and it will for you too. When you are at your lowest, you are not there forever. Take heart. Ahh . . . that takes us back to the scripture passage for today: do be strong and take heart for as you continue to hope and journey towards emotional healing, you will make it. **It can be a long climb to a summit, but it is worth it!**

Prayer

Lord, help all those who are reading about forgiveness this day. Maybe they forgive themselves, accept themselves, feel your presence, and gain a stronger hope and faith in the future. Help us all to journey to the summits you have for us. Continue to help us pamper ourselves as we heal that we may also be able to help others along the way. Teach us to enjoy the journey and not just cry out as to how long the journey may indeed take. Keep us moving. We pray with your strength and guidance. Amen.

Chapter End Projects

1) You must accept your past in order to heal. To deny it is to stuff and ignore. This does not work. Accept the past as there is nothing you can do about it. None of us can rewrite the past. Too bad. But we may actively scribe the present and dream for the future. We have discussed the past and accepting it before. What I suggest doing is writing a letter to your inner child. Say anything you want of course, but remember she is beautiful and she is you.

2) In this chapter, I gave a chart of what I saw as my levels to heal from the trauma. As stated earlier yours may be different and that is fine. For now, I suggest you mull these over and evaluate where you are at with these levels of the process. Do not worry if some are very difficult. Stage five of loving yourself can often be the hardest. Accept that it is a process.

	Stages	Is there work to be done in your heart for this to happen?
1	Accept your pain and suffering	
2	Accept that God allowed this to happen	
3	Know that God is with you	
4	Be patient with yourself as you process the pain	
5	Love yourself as you are	

6	In your heart, release the anger against the perpetrator	
7	In your mind, forgive him/her	
Possible 8	Meet with the perpetrator and forgive them so they could apologize to you if they are able and they could begin their own work	

3) How can you pamper your heart? How can you be the healing step today as you journey on? How can you possibly take heart?

4) I referenced Scrooge and the past, present, and future. If you were the principal character in a new "adapted version," where might God take you on the journey? What might be important to you? What about yourself would you like to change? Is there anyone you need to forgive? That could be yourself, or God, or people who didn't support you. This will take some time but it is valuable thinking.

 Tips for caregivers

1) Take some time to evaluate your own issues with forgiveness. What circumstances have affected you and have stunted growth in an area of your life? Or, is there someone upon reflection that you may have hurt? Or someone you no longer talk to because of conflict? Can you forgive yourself for mistakes made? Can you reach out to those who may be hurt and reconcile? This task is especially important for leaders and pastors as they have a higher level of responsibility as shepherds within God's flock.

2) So often we don't say sorry or ask for forgiveness as that is a sign of weakness. Compounding that in the last century is the fear that we could be prosecuted for our error as the law courts seem so busy with individuals seeking monetary

compensation for situations and actions that are hard to quantify. Ponder what your answers could be to questions of legal action. Your advice may be sought at various stages of the healing process.

PHASE FOREVER

Chapter 20

Molly's Moral
What Was the Purpose?

Psalm 34:1–9
I will extol the LORD at all times;
his praise will always be on my lips.
I will glory in the LORD;
let the afflicted hear and rejoice.
Glorify the LORD with me;
let us exalt his name together.
I sought the LORD, and he answered me;
he delivered me from all my fears.
Those who look to him are radiant;
their faces are never covered with shame.
This poor man called, and the LORD heard him;
he saved him out of all his troubles.
The angel of the LORD encamps around those who fear him,
and he delivers them.
Taste and see that the LORD is good;
blessed is the one who takes refuge in him.
Fear the LORD, you his holy people,
for those who fear him lack nothing.

Psalm 27:14
"Wait for the LORD;
be strong and take heart
and wait for the LORD."

Psalm 34

"Let the afflicted hear and rejoice" (Ps 34:2b). Wow! It doesn't say "after the afflicted are healed" they may rejoice. It says those who "are afflicted." The psalmist does not list what the affliction is, so it suggests to me at least a broad call for all who are suffering mentally or physically to hear the message of God and rejoice. In some translations, the word *afflicted* is translated as to be *humbled*. Yes, both physical and mental illness does humble one. **It is those who are at the opposite of feeling joy who are urged to rejoice and give thanks.** We have heard that in raising a child or working with employees that positive comments should outweigh negative by a tenfold margin. Those feeling depressed for whatever reason need joy, laughter, and the comfort of God to outweigh the negative feelings we have in the pit of despair. Sometimes one needs a role model for that. And that can tie into the theme of what was the purpose.

If Christians had a perfect life with no valleys to walk, no tunnels to guard, or no mountains to climb, how can we possibly help others if we cannot relate?

I echo what the psalmist has said for I too sought the Lord and He has healed my heart. He has given Molly the strength she needed to come forward, and in so doing, in His time, has healed her. Molly's adult has grown to love and accept her, and they exist together. (More about that in chapter 22.)

Another key verse in this Psalm is that "their faces are never covered in shame." When I was first engulfed in grief and shock over the abuse, the emotion that seemed to follow me everywhere was that of shame. I felt I had no worth. My self-confidence had been stolen, and I felt inadequate and somehow filthy. This psalmist says if we will look upon God, our faces will be shame free and somehow radiant. If we put God first, He will indeed be our comforter and we can then comfort others and bring them to the master physician.

Being able to thank God before the healing takes place comes only with a great inner strength, with time, with waiting upon God, and having role models to follow. The second half of Psalm 34 (not quoted above but I encourage you to read) is a sharing of wisdom from the psalmist's experience. Come and listen to me, David writes,

"The Lord is close to the brokenhearted and saves those who are crushed in spirit" (v. 34:18).

I was crushed and overwhelmed with dark emotions for many years. I don't know how a person without faith in God could make it through the healing of trauma from sexual abuse. I struggled to face the fears and found the courage to heal through God's word. Yes, I had friends that helped me, but I know it was my faith in God that did most the cleansing work in my heavy heart.

The Psalms are God inspired writings that are powerful for reading. God used the writing of those to provide hope and truth in the future. For example, this Psalm holds the verse that serves as prophecy that none of the bones of Jesus would be broken when He was crucified. The practice of breaking bones of those they crucified was to speed the process up. Jesus died quickly before that occurred. Match up with the Gospel of John (19:36) and you see the influence the book of Psalms had for the Jewish believer. There are also many prophetic words throughout the Old Testament that Jesus made sure to fulfil. The book of Psalms was and is more than light poetic reading. It is a lamp to light our path through all our journeys. **There is comfort and hope with God within the mud in our everyday lives.** That being the case, let us do as verse one says, to give God the praise continually. Many suffering around us need this hope, and many need to experience the peace of God in their troubled hearts.

So, you may say to yourself as you read the last few paragraphs, *"Oh yeah. Easy for her. As for me I don't know if I will ever be healed or ever thank God."* Let me say upfront I have probably been the slowest ever to catch on so do not feel badly. While it is easy for me now to recognize the great work that had happened over MANY years to heal heart and mind, being able to share about it has been one of the very last projects for me. It has felt so risky. I was afraid and probably will be again. Over time, however, I have had this burning to help others. How could I not? I thank God for His patience with me. I am smart in some things, but exceptionally slow in my mind in some others. Despite my struggles, God loves me and accepts me. He has put up with all my tears, and He has also dealt with my fears of publicly stating my struggles and the fact that I struggled, struggled, and struggled to achieve healing. But I am proud that I didn't bury my head in the sand. I did not bury Molly in a coffin but I have become friends with her. That was God. Totally. I thank Him. **I am no hero. I just ran the slowest marathon possible, but I completed that journey.**

Let me pass along to you an event from the life of Jesus that struck me anew in a book. Christine Caine recounts the story of Jesus taking a meager lunch and feeding the multitudes. What began as five loaves and two fish became an abundance to feed thousands. Please read some excerpts from this profound chapter in the book *Unstoppable*:

> *What are you facing that brings you face-to-face with your limitations, having you questioning how qualified you are to make a difference in this broken world?. . . Jesus accepted the five loaves and two fishes, small though they were. One packed lunch. A meager amount of food. It was all the boy had, but he offered it all . . . When the boy gave his little to Jesus, Jesus blessed it, and it became much in his hands . . . Do you know the first thing Jesus did with the meager offering? He looked up to heaven and gave thanks to God for the little he was given by the boy . . . Next, Jesus broke the bread and the fish. When he blessed it, there were five and two. But when he broke it, we lose count . . . **The miracle is in the breaking.**[65]*

The bolding above is mine. Caine goes on to remind readers that God uses our brokenness for His Glory. **I had not thought before of the miracle work of Christ coming through brokenness. That is a life-giving thought to ponder. Maybe we are best if broken?**

So back to the question of this chapter: What was the purpose? I expect you will find it is the question that keeps getting answered one small step at a time. You will understand it differently the longer your life journey progresses. Possible answers could be to draw you closer to God, to comfort others, or maybe it is to enliven your emotions and be more expressive. **The answer to the question of what was the purpose is not as important as the journey itself.** The most important is that God goes with you and He will rescue you from fear and give you peace. When one has been in a storm, one sees even better the beauty of the earth when the storm passes. Stop and give thanks no matter where you are in your journey.

> *Coming Out . . .*
> *Sexual abuse—a hush covers the space*
> *No one talks about sexual abuse.*
> *In the church, we can pray for the sick, the*
> *lost . . . but what do we do with the abused?*
> *Those who's most innermost part has been broken . . .*
> *Something meant for good has been stolen.*
> *There is pain, there is loss, there is grief . . .*
> *But those heavy hearts hide in the church*
> *They feel unworthy*
> *They feel second class*
> *They don't feel safe to talk*
> *Their hearts are often triggered   . . .*

... They learn to cover up, to stuff.
~~*The deepest pain and the least support.*~~
Where is the justice in that?
God loves those who are hurt,
but we need more than God,
we need more than the head of the body of Christ,
we need the rest of the body to care for us.
We need to be carried
Accepted . . . loved . . . prayed for . . . supported
Understood . . . healed . . . an equal in Christ

Why don't we share?
Easy: the church is more comfortable with the perfect Christian, loving, peaceful, giving, hospitable, secure, wealthy . . . those who look good inside and out. Isn't this backwards? Isn't the church a place to go for help?
Wasn't Christ an example of reaching out past the Jewish faith to the Gentile?
Reaching out to the sick and the weak and making them whole?
Christ gave himself for all, so why don't we do that in the church?

Why can't we extend a hand of acceptance, love and trust to those who are broken hearted . . . To those who from an early age have had their growth stunted.

They say one quarter of all females have been abused. That being the case why is it a secret in the church?
These people are in the church.
They need care but they don't have the courage to admit they need help.
How sad is this . . .
What is the answer? I have no idea, but I know I must do my part. I can see through the eyes of many. I can often see if they have been abused.
Lord, guide me to serve the wrongly assaulted!
Strengthen me that I might be able to come out and feel loved and accepted.

Communicating fully is the opposite of being traumatized. (Bessell van der Kolk)[66]

Prayer

Gracious God, thank you! Thank you for walking with me, for your patience, for your healing touch, for those you sent into my life to assist, and for helping me through the tunnel of shame out to the fields of beauty and peace.

For the many who read this book, may they gain a new hope for recovery. May they be reminded to focus on you, to wait patiently, and to thank you at all times. Help them be thankful and that joy leads to healing. Amen.

Chapter End Projects

1) Can you think of any answers to the question of what was the purpose for this struggle in your own life? Before you answer a quick no, I encourage you to stop and ponder. There is suffering in the world, and many varieties of suffering. If you know God loves you, then you must accept His journey and accept there is a purpose. It may take you a long time but ponder. It is possible the best outcome for you was to become an amazing writer without even knowing it but it developed through writing passionately in your journal. Take some time and think of three things you know that have improved in your life since you started this process. If you can't think of three, then keep working. If you have more than three just keep writing!

   *

   *

   *

2) Write a thank-you letter to God for work done and work you anticipate being done. When you have finished writing the letter, read it aloud and let the words penetrate both heart and mind. You can then come back to this letter and add items of thanksgiving each month. You will see in the next chapter I give you some ideas for why we should all be thankful, but come up with some now before you go on.

 Tips for caregivers

1) Often the hurting heart is too close to the pain to see any purpose. You, however, may be able to provide a lot of insight and meaning into the purpose for the journey. Help share this positive!

2) You also may be able to connect the life experience of the one you have journeyed with alongside another who may need similar help. This can be an important step in healing for all. Do this with prayer and wisdom.

Chapter 21

Molly's Melody
How Can I Thank the God
Who Restores Me?

> <u>Psalm 9:1–2</u>
> *"I will give thanks to you, LORD, with all my heart;*
> *I will tell of all your wonderful deeds.*
> *I will be glad and rejoice in you;*
> *I will sing the praises of your name, O Most High."*
>
> <u>Psalm 28:6–7</u>
> *"Praise be to the LORD,*
> *for he has heard my cry for mercy.*
> *The LORD is my strength and my shield;*
> *my heart trusts in him, and he helps me.*
> *My heart leaps for joy,*
> *and with my song I praise him."*

There are some words which seems so difficult yet they are foundational to all relationships. I would list the top three as *please, sorry,* and *thanks.* I may sound a bit like Ann Landers[67], but it is essential we all make a practice of using them. I will only deal with the need for thankfulness in this book and leave the others.

<u>Why I should be thankful:</u>

1. Every day is a gift of God.
2. We all live by grace.
3. I made it through the journey to the summit.

4. Molly has protected my heart very well.
5. I didn't get myself into trouble.
6. God provided great friends to see me through.
7. I have learned that waiting is worth it.
8. God also provided physical healing.
9. I am prepared to tell my story for others.
10. I don't need to hide.
11. I have grown much deeper in faith through all of this.
12. After much time, I have grown to appreciate my experience and love Molly.

Why I know you can be thankful:

1. You have been able to read this book.
2. You have a natural desire to search for solutions.
3. You can experience the same healing and grace from God.
4. There is more support for victims of abuse than ever before.
5. God is as close to you as your breath, so reach out and grab the master healer.
6. There are many books and counselors who can help you.

There are of course many other reasons why you can be thankful even if you have just started your journey!

Psalm 9:1–2 and Psalm 28:6–7

God hears our cries for help, and He is indeed faithful to answer. It is helpful to know that the psalmist struggled; for someone to say they are thankful yet have not struggled, their testimony isn't strong enough. Let's use money as an example. Those who may have inherited a lot of money may not appreciate the gift of a cup of coffee as much as the one who has little. The family who has been through bankruptcy and has started a second time in life successfully knows how fortunate they are as it is possible to fail. If all was good for the psalmists, or the other many strong biblical characters, they would not seem as human or as real. Stories of the struggle of others helps to validate our own experience.

Psalm 28 refers to some type of pit that psalmist was in. The pit was often a metaphor for death, and while we don't know the specific pit in this poem, it does suggest a significant event close to death rather than a slight fall into a crevasse. If we take the image of illness, when one has significant pain or injury and is then healed from it, the sense of relief is overwhelming. Verse 1 reveals there is a pit of some kind, and verse 2 lets us know that he called to God for help. When we arrive at verse 6, the psalmist knows his God has heard him and has given him reason to rejoice.

We often look at others and think their lives must be perfect, but we all struggle to different degrees and work hard to hide that struggle. Why? There are many answers to this, but I bring up one: we tend to be closed as people. We neither share the issues NOR share the celebration when we make it through. I challenge you to celebrate. The psalmist has a heart that leaps for joy (Psalm 28:7). That is a great image. When did you leap last for something other than a sports game? When did you last sing praises for what God has done?

I am reminded of the story of the ten lepers from Luke 17. They called for help, and Jesus told them to show themselves to the priests. One came back after being healed, and the amazing thing to me was that he was noted as a Samaritan. He was not Jewish but had the faith in the words of Jesus to go and show himself to the priest, whom he would not know, and he was healed. This might have been quite risky for him but worth the outcome. He was the only one to come back, but he had the highest risk in the process. That one leper was one who you would think would avoid the instruction as he would be entering a place of faith he was not familiar with. Jesus asked,

Were not all ten cleansed? Where are the other nine? Has no one returned to give praise to God except this foreigner? (Luke 17:17–18)

We hear nothing of the other nine, nor do we hear any further on the life of the Samaritan, but the message is that Jesus was surprised only one came back and set this one healed man as an example of faith. The grateful man returned to thank Jesus, and I remind you that he was a foreigner. The message of the healing would heighten the interest in this Jesus he would tell about. His healing would be an example to the non-Jewish world of the miracles of a living and loving God.

In all things give thanks

Really?
How?
Thanks for invasion of boundaries?
Thanks for pain and suffering?
Thanks for a dysfunctional family that couldn't protect me?
Thanks for being alone?

It has been a long process to be thankful.
I am now thankful for many things
and while my heart can't rejoice in thanksgiving for everything
I trust God is molding me for His purpose.
It will all make sense eventually!
He is in control
and for that I can indeed give thanks,
even if many details I can't be thankful for.

We all need an attitude of gratitude. This would change the world starting with those closest around us. How do you feel when you give a gift and don't get a thank-you? If it is an anonymous gift I can understand that, but is there an expectation that we should receive? There shouldn't be. We must be sincere in our thanks. It must come from our hearts, not out of a feeling of requirement. This is something that needs to be learned.

I have been on a long journey. There were bumps along the path, but I have come so far. I am fortunate. Because of my experiences, I have what I see as a real and close relationship with God. I am real. I don't cover up. (Well not too much anyhow.) I am happy to feel. I am thankful to experience life without a weight on my shoulders.

I am thankful to God for faithfulness. Even when I felt God was not near, our gracious and loving God was very close! I am also thankful to my small network of Molly support team friends who stood by me faithfully. As I have grown in my understanding, I am also thankful to Molly. Yes, she used to keep me up at night, but I have learned so much from her. She has carried the weight of heaviness, and now I can carry her and walk with her.

> *Thanks to the inner child*
> *I have questioned why you were silent . . .*
> *I have questioned why there are memory gaps . . .*
> *I confess I have been angry with you at times.*
> *I am sorry inner child.*
> *I know now you were protecting me,*
> *caring for me and sheltering my heart.*
> *Because of your strength, I have been successful:*
> *educated*
> *employable*
> *Thank you!*
> *Help me know how to care for you now.*
> *Speak that I might hear you clearly.*

Healing is feeling my story as beautiful despite all the pain and struggle.[68] (Jane Rowan)

Rowan's quote about seeing one's story as beautiful is after a very long path and lots of pondering time for all of us. I expect the first time I read it I would have been inclined to decide there would be no hope to healing for my heart as it is difficult to see the positive amid crisis. Yet, time heals wounds for sure. In years past, I would not want my story told but I am building more courage with each spoken story. I have a stronger passion to help others.

<u>Ways I can thank God</u>:

Spend time with God regularly
Help others who are in my situation
Help others financially
Dedicate my time to doing His work
Celebrate God's work in my life with others
Write the rest of this book (getting closer as this is chapter 21)
Trust God as we continue to journey together
Speak out for those who may have lost their voice
Develop my gifts better
Care for myself

Prayer

Thank you, Gracious God, for healing. I thank you for the inner child who has protected me for years, for the adult who was ready to begin the journey, and for your guidance as we travelled. It was not always easy, but we have done it with the help of many others. Thank you for my support team, thank you for strength and keeping me safe. Guide us as we seek to share thankfulness and help others along the way. Amen.

Chapter End Projects

1) How can you thank your inner child for being strong? She stuffed her heart until you were ready. She was strong until you were strong enough to care for her. She waited until you had enough time to wait. Thank her for her wisdom!

2) How can you thank God through your life?

3) What have you learned about being thankful in all things?

4) Find a Bible and read Philippians 4:4–8. This contains closing thoughts from Paul to the church in Philippi that he thanked God for every time he thought of them (Phil. 1:3-6).

 Tips for caregivers

1) Thank God for the many you have had the privilege to help, and thank God for the learning you have experienced as a mentor. Your life has been changed for the better in service to God. Thank God for that as well.

Chapter 22

Molly and Me
How Can I Praise the Creator?

> *Psalm 100*
> *"Shout for joy to the LORD, all the earth.*
> *Worship the LORD with gladness;*
> *come before him with joyful songs.*
> *Know that the LORD is God.*
> *It is he who made us, and we are his;*
> *we are his people, the sheep of his pasture.*
> *Enter his gates with thanksgiving*
> *and his courts with praise;*
> *give thanks to him and praise his name.*
> *For the LORD is good and his love endures forever;*
> *his faithfulness continues through all generations."*

It is a relief to have weight taken off your shoulders when you are on any journey. Again, think of a heavy backpack as you hike up a mountain. You become tired, and so a friend takes your pack to assist your climb. That gift of help allows you to catch your breath, move with more ease, and reach your goal sooner than you may have thought. If you haven't been in that situation, or one like it, you might not understand what a relief unloading stress can be.

> *Mountain Climbing*
> *The mountains are beautiful*
> *majestic*
> *inspiring*
> *Yet if they could talk they would have stories of the*
> *pain of bursting forth in their creation: the noise,*
> *the shaking of the earth . . . dramatic change.*
> *We now long to go to the mountains to breathe the fresh*
> *air, to smell the woods, to see the wild animals, to see*
> *the bursts of grass through a crevasse in the rock . . .*
> *We long to climb; a climb that we must do in our hearts:*
> *there is pain*
> *great confusion*
> *change*
> *Yet at the end of the process we can stand tall as a mountain*
> *and provide a place of solace for other troubled souls.*
> *Carry on then...climb the mountain and complete*
> *the journey for yourself and for others.*

In the early pages of this book, you read about my serious illness as a child but I gave few specifics. I had picked up encephalitis (inflammation of the brain) and had caught it most likely from a mosquito. I was paralyzed on my right side and in a coma for a few weeks. The doctors suggested to my parents that the minister from our United Church come and pray, as it was assumed I would not make it through. I did live obviously, but I was left with debilitating headaches that caused me to spend great amounts of time in the hospital through my preteen years. My parents were told part of my brain was black from the illness, meaning it was dead. They were also told over the years not to expect me to ever make it through high school, either because I would lack IQ ability or not live that long. Fascinating, isn't it? I am thankful to have proved them all wrong.

When my dad was suffering from what they called mild dementia, they took some pictures of his brain and reported on visual evidence of brain damage. That got me thinking . . . in thirty years or more when I am a senior, in the hospital, and they decide something is wrong with my brain, I could be in trouble. What happens if they take a scan of my brain and realize some is missing? They don't have a benchmark to know this has been my normal condition and I could be put into a lockdown ward for being as I have been my whole life. Yikes.

In the fall of 2015, my current doctor and I decided it would be good to have a wee check to see what the gray matter looked like. I was nervous as you can imagine! The excellent news was there was no evidence of brain damage. My illness happened at a young enough age that brain recovery could happen and obviously did. Thank God for that! No doubt the many early years were times of healing and resetting networks. My music training no doubt helped a lot. There is still residual evidence of illness but not in my brain; it is the nerve connection from right foot to brain that didn't recover, but the signals from brain to foot are fine. This has accounted for several bad falls and a lot of foot pain, but now that I understand one foot doesn't respond correctly I am much more careful!

So this chapter is "Molly and Me," and we both have a lot to celebrate! Molly has come out of the trunk, said what she needed to, and has felt love and acceptance from her adult. Her adult is celebrating as well. She has understood the shame of abuse and made it through carrying her inner child for many years until she was strong enough to be an equal and be as one with her. And, it turns out that while Molly was hiding her pain, God was using the amazing healing aspects to bring physical healing. Both Molly and her adult have a lot to celebrate, but it has taken so many years to work through so many things. There was a long wait for resolution and healing, but God is faithful and His love has indeed been very present in my life.

This next picture is one of many from the recent MRI I had to set a baseline brain function for the future, for my senior moments as they will be called I am sure. (Fig22:1). Look both sides are working just great!

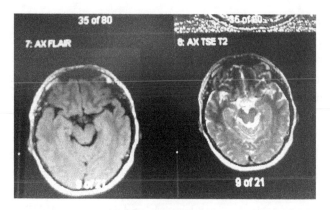

Figure 22:1 Proof of God's healing power!

I am not a doctor and have no clue how to read any of these things, but look carefully at the image on the left. It almost looks like a happy face. In fact, it looks more like a happy dog face (see Figure 22:2 for comparison), but I take it is a happy brain smiling at me! See the similarity below!

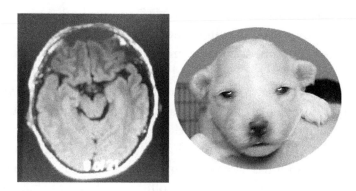

Figure 22:2: A new puppy on the right with eyes just open. If she were smiling, she resembles the pic of my brain quite nicely! This is called looking for the smile in all things!

Molly and I press on with our journey as one. We both feel encouraged and strengthened. We have been through many things and have the strength to let others know they can make it through as well. We have seen God at work for us, and through the lives of those He sent to help us as well.

Psalm 100

The NIV translation starts Psalm 100 with "shout for joy." I first learned this Psalm as a youth in the King James Version, which starts "make a joyful noise." I have always preferred that phrase. I was born into a family with a very musical mom, and my older sister who did well in music. The three of us would all list music as our main profession. Then there was dad . . . we usually asked him not to sing. It was to him, though, that this Psalm could have been written and a reminder to me of many things:

1) It doesn't matter how we thank him that we just need to.
2) A joyful noise says nothing about being in tune or well-rehearsed.
3) This noise is to be sincere and given as an offering.

Those with the gift of music can bring their gift at its best, but we need to remember that others may just have noise and we need to accept their offerings to God as just as important. God wants to hear a shout and a fanfare. We have higher expectations most times, but the means is not as important as the message. God is indeed amazing, and we need to rejoice and let the world know God has been great in our lives.

We have been created to worship God and to serve him with our lives. We are to serve the Lord with gladness and sing before Him. Music is a calling for all. Often in our churches, we see those who find the music portions a drag and they don't sing. The Jewish and Christian cultures all sing. We know the Levites were a chosen group of people whose role was to serve in the temple and play music. They were responsible day and night, so these musicians were exempt from other duties (see 1 Chronicles 9:28–33). They worked full time in the service of the temple. We also know that David played a harp and sang, and the Psalms written were sung poetry. We read in Matthew

26 that Jesus sang a hymn before they went to the Mount of Olives just after Jesus confronted Judas for being the traitor among them. Singing and making music is an important response in the Bible and for us. It is also both an individual and corporate activity.

What is it that we sing? That is outlined for us as well: we give thanks to God because He is good, faithful, and He loves us. It is hard for the hurt heart to accept love, so we may find it difficult in our early stages of healing to recognize God's work of healing through others to us. We also may not be able to see His faithful hand in our lives, but it is important to stop and give thanks when you are aware of something to thank him for. Make a joyful noise! Find some recordings you can sing along with that share testimonies of praise. Sing Christmas carols loudly when you hear them being played in the background when you are out shopping. Join a choir or learn an instrument. There is a lot of research as to the health benefits of music from improved breathing to increased brain activity. I encourage you to follow the instruction to make a joyful noise to serve God. You don't need music lessons to do this, but if you happen to fall in love with this artistic means of expression, then seek out a coach.

So make a joyful noise. Today and always!

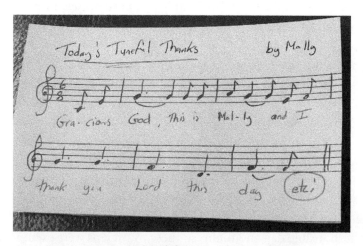

Figure 22:3: A thankful tune from Molly . . .
simple and just perfect in God's eyes.

Prayer

Gracious God, I praise you for your faithfulness to me and your love for me. You are the creator of my life, and you walk beside me through all things. Thank you. Thank you. Thank you. Make my life an offering of praise to you for what you have done in my life. Teach me to serve you in song, and help me shout out to the world of your loving kindness so others may see you. Use my life as an inspiration to others. Amen.

Chapter End Projects

1) You are on a journey. You may travel some of the same paths over again in the future as you discover other peaks to climb, but you have journeyed and you can and should celebrate. Hopefully you prepared a party pack with you for the celebration! In many other things in life we throw a party: birthdays, baptisms, graduations (and even from kindergarten now!), engagements, weddings, promotions, competitions, house warmings, etc. It is time to celebrate you and your journey. Celebrate somehow and make sure you give our God who has walked with you the thanks for journeying with you.

So let's plan:

Where might you hold this event: _____
What would you do at it: _____
How could you be a role model to others through this event: _____
_____
Would you send people home with any party favors as a sign of hope and remembrance? _____
_____
What can you call this event (You may need to be creative here as most people don't hold healing socials for their inner child!) _____
_____

2) Project one is to plan a party, and this next project is to work on your invite list. Who has helped you in this journey? Maybe some have helped you and they do not even know they were role models for you. Invite them and encourage them. Share the joy! Maybe you need to invite

some who need to get on their own journey, and this would inspire them.

3) As part of your thankfulness, if you are able make a financial donation as a thank offering for God's work in your life: it could be to a women's shelter, a counseling center or a church as examples only of course. Share your joy!

 Tips for caregivers

1) Celebrate. Host a party.
2) Mark the occasion of recovery in some way.

Chapter 23

Meaning for Molly
What Can I Do to Help?

Psalm 116
"I love the LORD, for he heard my voice;
he heard my cry for mercy.
Because he turned his ear to me, I will
call on him as long as I live.
The cords of death entangled me, the
anguish of the grave came over me;
I was overcome by distress and sorrow.
Then I called on the name of the LORD: "LORD, save me!"
The LORD is gracious and righteous;
our God is full of compassion.
The LORD protects the unwary; when I
was brought low, he saved me.
Return to your rest, my soul, for the
LORD has been good to you.
For you, LORD, have delivered me from
death, my eyes from tears,
my feet from stumbling, that I may walk before
the LORD in the land of the living.
I trusted in the LORD when I said, "I am greatly afflicted";
in my alarm I said "Everyone is a liar."
What shall I return to the LORD
for all his goodness to me?
I will lift up the cup of salvation and
call on the name of the LORD. ...*

> *... I will fulfill my vows to the LORD*
> *in the presence of all his people.*
> *Precious in the sight of the LORD is the*
> *death of his faithful servants.*
> *Truly I am your servant, LORD; I serve*
> *you just as my mother did;*
> *you have freed me from my chains.*
> *I will sacrifice a thank offering to you and*
> *call on the name of the LORD.*
> *I will fulfill my vows to the LORD in*
> *the presence of all his people,*
> *in the courts of the house of the LORD—*
> *in your midst, Jerusalem.*
> *Praise the LORD."*

The longer and deeper the journey, the more I have learned of course, but not just about me. I have learned that God is indeed faithful and that I at times need the perspective of many years and hindsight to see that more clearly. I have also learned that experiencing sorrow, grief, and even confusion one learns more about themselves but also about God. I have learned also that the text from Romans 8:28 is indeed true, that "**we know that in all things God works for the good of those who love him, who have been called according to his purpose**." With short-term vision, we may not see the good, but God is working and does truly care for us. It is in waiting upon God that we learn of Him and that He gives us the wings to fly as eagles (Isaiah 40:31) and that with those wings we are to see the needs of others and help them. I have not been healed for my own good and purpose. Sure I benefit, but to not reach out by taking risks of openly sharing as well as taking the time to write this book, I am being self-ish. It is important for me to pause and thank God for His mercies and share those blessings with others.

Not all of you may be called to take a year off and write a book, but you will be called to other things. You may come alongside others who are hurting. You may take up a career in counseling or minis-try. You may volunteer at the local sexual assault safe house in your community. You may help fundraise for important areas of mental health. No matter what, you have been given the tools to help others. There is no rush as there isn't an expiry date, and you need to make sure you are healthy and strong as there will be people who question your story and possibly even your intentions. There are many ways you can help. Keep your gaze focused on the work of God and the people who need to meet His healing touch.

Nobody escapes being wounded. We are all wounded people, whether physically, emotionally, mentally, or spiritually. The main question is not, "How can we hide our wounds?" so we don't have to be embarrassed, but "How can we put our woundedness in the service of others?" When our wounds cease to be a source of shame, and become a source of healing, we have become wounded healers.[69] (Henri Nouwen)

Psalm 116

This Psalm is a thanksgiving for deliverance. It could have been deliverance from illness hinted at in verse 2 or possibly from people who have lied as seen in verse 11. Whatever the specific cause the author of this Psalm was troubled, he prayed for help and received it. This theme appears in many psalms, but this Psalm also features the desire to serve God and offer himself as an offering. What can I do to repay you for your help is the question posed?

The psalm is a part of the collection of psalms running from 113 to 118, called the "Egyptian Hallel" (Egyptian praise), centering on the story of the deliverance from Egypt. Psalm 113 is a hymn. Psalm 114 is the centerpiece of this collection, reporting the event of the exodus. As the central act of God's saving activity, the exodus is to the Old Testament what the cross-resurrection is to the New Testament. Psalm 115 then celebrates this event with a call to praise. Psalm 114 thus tells the story of the nation's deliverance from bondage and is followed by words of praise (Psalm 115:1, 18). Psalm 116 now tells the story of an individual's deliverance from death, and again is followed by words of praise, in Psalm 117. Psalm 116 also

*plays a part in the yearly biblical readings of Christian churches,
appearing in the ABC lectionary readings and also a text for Maundy
Thursday. Luke 22:14–23 and the parallels tell of Jesus celebrating
a meal with his disciples at Passover time. Psalm 116 would have
been sung as part of their Passover celebration.*[70] (James Limburg)

Psalm 116 as stated above was well known to the Jewish believers. It would have been spoken or read by Jesus himself in the celebration of Passover with His disciples the night before he died. Jesus came as the great servant of God and people, and He gave the ultimate sacrifice of his life. He also vowed the night before he was crucified to be faithful and fulfill the mission he was sent to earth for through the reading of these verses from Psalm 116. **Jesus gave us the best gift of all—his life for ours**.

Jesus was a Jew, and this Psalm was part of his faith foundation. The Old Testament was filled with prophecies about Him, and because of that we should do our best to learn of the history of God's dealings with His people. Jesus knew the scriptures well and often quoted from them. That would be to our advantage as well.

Back to Psalm 116 and the idea of making an offering to God for His deliverance. How we live our lives is a great testimony of what we see as important. I scribbled a quote down many years ago that is attributed to Oprah: "What we dwell on is who we become."[71] If we focus on God, we can live in this world that needs to see God in human form through us. If I give God my time and attention, I will be better able to serve Him.

The world is in need. My heart aches at the statistics that one in four women are abused. That number is so high. Think of your workplace, your college or university, your family, your church, and your friends. So many hurting people. All this pain I have experienced has been the experience of so many others. How can I help? How can God use my story to help others? I have a story of deliverance from trauma, and my sharing of that will help others. This is my way to serve: to speak to the many whose hearts ache, to those who may feel abandoned by people, the church and God as I did at many points of my journey with Molly. I will do the best I can with writing, with connecting, and I will leave the work of healing those I encounter to the Spirit of God. I know my journey will help some others, and that will bring meaning and fulfillment to my story. I will give all glory to our Gracious God.

> *How do we feel God's love?*
>
> *We can know God,*
> *We can see God,*
> *But how do we feel the love of God?*
> *From His people!*
> *That means we have a role to play:*
> *We must share*
> *We are God's hands and feet*
> *We are the way to reach out and touch the*
> *broken heart and give God's healing.*
> *We are vessels of God's Holy Spirit—the Master Comforter.*
> *Be ye filled and ready to serve.*

This next prayer from a journal comes near the completion of the journey.

> September 26, 2012
>
> Jesus hold my heart, draw me close to you,
> that I might heal to serve you better.
>
> Allow my experience to be a blessing to
> someone to help restore them.
> I desire to trade these sorrows in, and
> exchange them for the ability
> to love and care for others.
>
> Help me lay the burden aside, not that I forget,
> but that I may assist others to lay their burdens
> at the foot of your cross, Lord Jesus.
>
> Guide me, transform for your purpose!
> Amen

> **God does not comfort us to make us comfortable**
> **but to make us comforters.**
> (J.H. Jowett)[72]

Biographies are powerful tools for our growth. Through them we discover stories of others that intersect with paths in our stories. We are all on journeys with God through our lives, and anything we can do to help move others forward is a good thing. Remember that you must come first in the healing process. I am reminded of airline safety instructions as we prepare for liftoff: secure the oxygen mask on your face before you help others around you. They don't say, of course, that not doing that could kill both you and your child, as you don't want to be overwhelmed with fear. As you carry on your journey to recovery, remember to take baby steps that keep you feeling safe. Your inner child has not walked as much as you, so small steps and short distances are the best to start. Molly and I had a slow journey, but the turtle can indeed finish the race! It is a journey of waiting, being still, learning to trust, and learning to love yourself again.

Prayer

Healing God, we come to you in celebration of life, of choices we can make, and your willingness to let us grow and develop into the people you desire each of us to be. Mold us into the vessels for the Holy Spirit You desire us to be. Fill us to overflowing that we may spread the good news of restoration and salvation to those who need it. Remind each of us to walk beside you, grasping onto your hand always and not racing ahead with no plan.

Thank you, God, for your love, your faithfulness, your care, your healing touch, and your grace. Amen.

Chapter End Projects

1) Let's get creative! There are so many ways God could use you for His work here on earth. The number of suffering people does not seem to shrink no matter how many advances we made with technology or learning. So, I challenge you to step out and try something very different, just to do it. Take a craft class, decide to paint a picture, join a choir, start curling, or plant a garden. Try a few things to build your confidence that you can do something new and that it is even fun. You will build new friendships and try out your new wings!

2) As God is molding and shaping you, step out to see how you can change the shape of the neighborhood around you that it may become a better place. We all have gifts within us, and many of these talents lie dormant because of fear. I recall a passage in 2 Timothy 1:6 which encourages all people to fan the flame of the gifts you have within you. I am not suggesting you become a pyromaniac and light unsuitable fires that cause harm and damage in real life, of course. I am suggesting that you have been gifted by God, and if you stir that fire a bit—through prayer and trying new things—you may have new avenues open up for your future. That can be exciting and rewarding.

3) Ask others who know you well what they think you might be good at doing as a volunteer an evening a week, or in transition to a new job. These friends of yours may have no ideas or you may end up with a collection of options that you could never accomplish in one lifetime. Remember it is always good to live with an open mind of what God can do through you. These are suggestions only, and you and God may of course work to find what the best solution for you is. Enjoy this step and enjoy new things!

Tips for caregivers

1) You can help be a bridge to future goals. Once you are confident that healing has taken place and restoration made, then you can help make the transition from victim to mentor.

Conclusion

This book has been a journey for me to write and, I expect, for you to read. The most intense journey is of course the long path from brokenness and through awareness, from shame through acceptance, to understanding and healing. We all walk a different path, and your story will be different than mine, as it should be. I have attempted to share enough of my story that you see that I understand through personal experience and that I have hit speed bumps and walls. I have also questioned myself, God, and everyone in-between. Sorry, everyone. I have made it, and you can as well with patience, self-acceptance, and willingness to accept love from others and to love yourself as God's unique and beautiful creation.

While the twenty-three chapters were assigned themes and scripture passages back in 2011, I left the conclusion until the book was nearing completion and my true healing was confident. Shifting from the usual chapter outline, I will explain why the chosen psalm is meaningful to me first and then let you read the psalm.

Psalm 91

While many feel this Psalm was written by David based on similarities to other writings, there is no proof which in many ways allows us to free the story line from the specific dangers and trials in David's life if he was the author.

This Psalm divides itself nicely into three themes:

a) a **personal declaration of trust** in God who has been a refuge and shelter in great stress (91:1–2),
b) the equivalent of a mini sermon/pep talk as to **why everyone should trust** God (91:3–13), and

c) a **response from God** promising to provide protection and salvation (91:14–16).

One of the commentaries I read highlighted four metaphors used in this Psalm to describe divine protection[73].

Metaphor Used	Representative Trait of God
Shelter	A hiding place safe from evil and fear
Shadow	Used with shadow of thy wings, like a mother bird protecting her young
Refuge	A place of retreat that provides a haven of rest for the heart
Fortress	Strength and grandeur needed to withstand even the strongest battles

The element of trust is one of the most difficult obstacles for the abused. It has been mine. The image of hiding in a sheltered spot of a mother's wings in Psalm 91 reminds me of Isaiah 40:31: "Those who hope in the Lord will renew their strength. They will soar on wings like eagles, they will run and not grow weary, they will walk and not be faint." The translation I have memorized uses "wait upon the Lord" rather than "hope in the Lord." I prefer the idea of waiting. In the instruction to wait before being able to soar, I am reminded of two important thoughts:

1) We are encouraged to wait. But there are no stipulations to that waiting. There is no timeline or schedule to meet, so you do not have to "heal in a certain time" or be frustrated by "friends" who feel your journey is too long. For some people, waiting may be longer than you would expect, so those around you may have to learn to wait as well. If they truly love you, they will not grow impatient.

2) Waiting reminds me also of the story of the tortoise and the hare, one of Aesop's Fables. While there have been many

interpretations, some even including trickery and dishonesty to win the race, the idea I want to encourage you with is the notion that slow and steady does indeed win the race. See the image and quote below:[74]

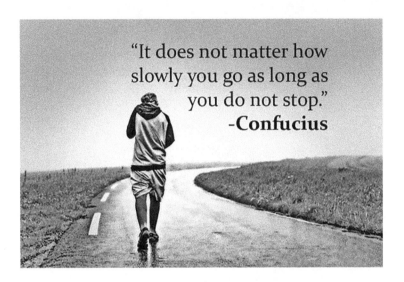

"It does not matter how slowly you go as long as you do not stop."
-Confucius

We are called to live each day as a gift, and in our journey, we only need to be in motion to be progressing. The speed of that journey and healing has no time schedule. Be patient with yourself. The more you can accept and love yourself, the sooner you will be soaring with wings as an eagle rather than plodding like any poor turtle. As noted at the end of Psalm 91, God will be with you. He has been for me, and I am thankful for the healing I have experienced. It has freed me to accept myself and live life in the present with a positive vision of the future.

The reading of Psalm 91 is next. Read the verses aloud, ponder, repeat. Know that the author, whoever that is, is speaking from experience. Our role is to trust and love God our creator. We will not understand His workings in and through our lives, but we can take refuge that He is nearer to us than we can ever imagine.

> *Psalm 91*
> *He who dwells in the shelter of the Most High*
> *will rest in the shadow of the Almighty.*
> *I will say of the LORD, "He is my refuge and*
> *my fortress, my God, in whom I trust."*
> *Surely he will save you from the fowler's*
> *snare and from the deadly pestilence.*
> *He will cover you with his feathers, and under*
> *his wings you will find refuge; his faithfulness*
> *will be your shield and rampart.*
> *You will not fear the terror of night, nor the arrow*
> *that flies by day, nor the pestilence that stalks in the*
> *darkness, nor the plague that destroys at midday.*
> *A thousand may fall at your side, ten thousand at*
> *your right hand, but it will not come near you.*
> *You will only observe with your eyes and*
> *see the punishment of the wicked.*
> *If you make the Most High your dwelling—even*
> *the LORD, who is my refuge then no harm will*
> *befall you, no disaster will come near your tent.*
> *For he will command his angels concerning*
> *you to guard you in all your ways;*
> *they will lift you up in their hands, so that you*
> *will not strike your foot against a stone.*
> *You will tread upon the lion and the cobra; you*
> *will trample the great lion and the serpent.*
> *"Because he loves me," says the LORD, "I will rescue*
> *him; I will protect him, for he acknowledges my name.*
> *He will call upon me, and I will answer him; I will be*
> *with him in trouble, I will deliver him and honor him.*
> *With long life will I satisfy him and show him my salvation."*

Prayer

Gracious God, thank you that you do shelter and protect us. That you guide every moment and that we live to reflect your beauty and grace. Thank you for loving us and healing us when we felt downtrodden. May we continue to walk boldly with you and remind us to rest in you at the end of each day. Amen.

Coda: Musings

Musicians will recognize the term *coda* that translates as "tail." It refers to an extra bit added to the end a composition that isn't needed for the piece to feel complete but provides length, repetition, or sometimes another thought entirely. Most authors choose to use an appendix format for extra information relating to the chapters. This coda material as I present to you is not directly a part of the healing journey but more informative regarding the external process one faces in a situation of abuse. It seemed most fitting for me to leave it at the "outside" of the book as a coda. It is also directed to caregivers as they ponder what to do with information passed along to them.

1) <u>Reporting abuse</u>

We have a legal responsibility to protect children and youth considered under legal age. We need to speak for them and report situations of abuse. (*Make sure you know the facts first so as not to create unnecessary issues of course! One does have to be cautious as there could be significant retaliations for wrongful accusations.*)

Those who are sexually abused at any age may and should consider a report. Perpetrators seldom have just one victim. Apparently, there is a sense of power over the victim, and this is a thrill (somehow) to the mind of a rapist. If they feel secure they have enough control over their victims, they will feel they are free to repeat the actions with others and not be discovered. You will have noted many instances of this in the news.

We may feel we are protecting someone by not reporting, but we also may cause the pain of another. Wisdom is needed in this process. Remember there is no rush except to protect and care for the one whom you know is being abused. Take someone out of a situation if you have any concern that further injury could be done. This could mean moving them out of the house, job situation, or possibly locating to a different area of the city until the victim has time to process and recover. Communication channels are essential in this stage, however, so you are not charged with kidnapping!

2)   Follow through: what to do?

Your response needs time and careful thinking. There is no rush in follow up once the victim is protected from further stress, but I offer you some tips from my own thinking through the years. If you choose to proceed with more than just basic charges, a lawyer's advice is most worthwhile. You must be ready to pay some costs that may not be covered the moment you enter the law office door, but their thoughts would be most valuable on many counts. Laws vary from place to place, and laws also change based on other cases that have been tried.

There are three broad options for follow-through after initial charges, but there could be slight deviations of these of course.

a)   The matter can be settled out of court
b)   You may decide not to follow through with a lawsuit, but the perpetrator will have a criminal record
c)   You may decide to take the perpetrator through the court process at which time all can become a segment of the public news

I did not take Molly and myself through any steps listed above, but that does not serve as the example for everyone for sure. That is why this information is a coda and not an appendix of the main book itself where I share through the book of Psalms from my heart, mind, and experience. These are my musings which may be useful in your situation. I again encourage you to seek out advice from others.

Let me start the thoughts in the coda as I have done through the book with scripture:

> *Psalm 39:1–3*
> *I said, "I will watch my ways*
> *and keep my tongue from sin;*
> *I will put a muzzle on my mouth*
> *as long as the wicked are in my presence."*
> *But when I was silent and still,*
> *not even saying anything good,*
> *my anguish increased.*
> *My heart grew hot within me,*
> *And as I meditated, the fire burned;*
> *Then I spoke with my tongue . . .*

Vengeance . . . revenge, punishment, retribution, and retaliation. The author writes in this Psalm that fires can burn inside if not dealt with. Anguish will grow, not lessen. One of the aims of counseling is to verbalize. Being silent is not the answer to resolution. Communication of some form is imperative whether it be to someone else in a private room that you trust with your secrets or in a public space at the local law courts building. Knowing which form of communication is best for your personal healing is the purpose of thoughts on these concluding pages.

We often turn our anger, as the psalms often do, to the enemy or in our case the perpetrator, which is indeed part of the process of realization and healing. Anger is also a healthy stage of grief noted by the author Elisabeth Kübler-Ross.[75] True if the abuser hadn't made a poor decision, we wouldn't be writing or reading this book! We need to do the resolution of the conflict ourselves.

How many people have you known that have gone through the judicial system only to be disappointed and exhausted by the outcome? No jury whether favorable or not to your purpose ever repairs the damage done. For example, there could be mistakes made in the process and the abuser can be set free of all charges and have their slate wiped clean although they may carry guilt! All the public sharing of one's heart for nothing can be devastating and life altering in its own way. Make sure you do not go to the court assuming a win will bring healing. Very few cases of abuse can be proved, and the perpetrators usually go free. This can create even further hurt for the victim.

In Canadian law, there is no statute of limitations on sexual abuse. That means at any time a victim may press charges, there is no safety valve for perpetrators. In my situation, by the time my sub-conscious recalled the events, the doctor in question was no longer working because of his age, was near death, and has now since died. I had obtained very superficial information that there had been official complaints made against the doctor, but these were not public files and I didn't proceed on any action.

What I could have done:

1) Obtained a lawyer and filed for damages based on the effect this had on my life to cover costs. I have paid an emotional price for sure, and that has had practical con-sequences. I am single and not by choice but most likely of fear. Maybe I could have "made some money," but that doesn't change the situation for me. Money doesn't heal the wounded heart or body, although it may allow for more comfort and relief.

2) If the doctor was still working, pressing charges is some-thing I may have done to stop others from possibly going through the same situation. It appears others who were not as stuffed as me were able to do that. You will have heard of situations where a celebrity has an accusation made and then many more come forward. In some situations, this can be very helpful as you develop a community to care for each other. But winning these cases is most difficult. There is a cost of time, expense, privacy, etc. If there is public awareness, hopefully the rapist won't repeat their actions, but . . .

Yes, we have reason to be angry and upset, as we were violated. We need to protect others from being hurt for sure, but does retalia-tion in whatever form help us? Is vengeance useful? Is suing for wrongdoings vengeance or not? And how does that tie in with the Christian call for forgiveness? I have more questions than answers! Sorry.

This has been a book about God's work in our lives and our hearts. I turn back to the knowledge that in the end God is supreme judge. It is God who holds all to account for wrongdoings. We must work at trying to live lives that reflect the love of God and work on developing our own faith. No matter how you follow up legally with the abuser, you will still have your own work to do in reconciliation, which is purpose of the bulk of the book. Be patient, take time, and care for yourself at all times as you are worth it and have value!

I close this coda to the book with a message from Paul's letter to the Romans. May it serve as a guide as you journey yourself, and as you decide what the best course of action is for yourself. Each of us have a different path. I have shared my journey and what I have seen along the way. You will have a different map for a different journey. Key for the journey is that we are to love ourselves, others, and our creator.

> *Romans 12:9–21*
> *Love must be sincere. Hate what is evil; cling to what is good. Be devoted to one another in brotherly love. Honor one another above yourselves. Never be lacking in zeal, but keep your spiritual fervor, serving the Lord. Be joyful in hope, patient in affliction, faithful in prayer. Share with God's people who are in need. Practice hospitality.*
>
> *Bless those who persecute you; bless and do not curse. Rejoice with those who rejoice; mourn with those who mourn. Live in harmony with one another. Do not be proud, but be willing to associate with people of low position. Do not be conceited.*
>
> *Do not repay anyone evil for evil. Be careful to do what is right in the eyes of everybody. If it is possible, as far as it depends on you, live at peace with everyone. Do not take revenge, my friends, but leave room for God's wrath, for it is written: "It is mine to avenge; I will repay," says the Lord. On the contrary: "If your enemy is hungry, feed him; if he is thirsty, give him something to drink. In doing this, you will heap burning coals on his head." Do not be overcome with evil, but overcome evil with good.*

Psalm Use Index

I read the Psalms in their entirety a few times while working on the original outline of *The Molly Project*. You will see that twenty-seven were used in part or the whole to speak to various stages of the journey Molly travelled. I have included this index for those that may be interested in their own study.

Psalm Number	Chapter Referenced
4	4
6	14
9	21
10	4
12	5
13	11
18	15
25	10
	13
27	20
28	21
30	6
31	1
	19
33	18
34	2
	20
35	3
37	7
	16
39	Coda
42	12
51	17

End Notes

1   Zelinski, Ernie J. "How to retire happy, wild and free" Visions International Publishing, 2014, p. 71.

2   *Brainyquotes*: http://www.brainyquote.com/quotes/topics/topic_patience.html Accessed December 2016

3   *Goodreads.com quotes:* http://www.goodreads.com/quotes/82878-i-must-be-willing-to-give-up-what-i-am This quote I first saw many years ago in a weekly calendar, and I copied it onto a green index card that I kept looking at as a reminder to tackle the book project. It is one of many great Albert Einstein quotes. End notes citation accessed February 1, 2017

4   *The Life Recovery Bible* Tyndale House Publishers, 1992, p. 610.

5   Crabb, Dr. Larry *Inside Out* Navpress Publishing Group, 1988, p. 32. This book by Dr. Crabb deals with varied mental issues and not exclusively with sexual abuse. It is an interesting read although as a Lutheran I needed to use eyeglasses of God's grace to filter some of the comments.

6   http://www.christian-lyrics.net/laura-story/blessings-lyrics.html#axzz4o3EcX84A. Accessed on line July 27, 2017

7   http://www.newreleasetoday.com/article.php?article_id=551. Accessed July 27, 2017. Her story includes a brain tumor her husband had. Her faith strengthened her to carry on.

8   *Bell let's talk mental health*: http://letstalk.bell.ca/en/our-initiatives/_Accessed from an interview given in January 2016

9   Van der Kolk, Bessel A. *The Body Keeps Score* Penguin Books, 2014, p. 2.

10   https://www.google.ca/search?q=free+pictures+of+mazes+and+the+letter+m&rlz=1C1MSNA_enCA705CA705&tbm=isch&tbo=u&source=univ&sa=X&ved=0ahUKEwigu5ybuKzVAhWm34MKHTGTAHQQ7AkIOA&biw=1536&bih=735#im

grc=9WusLc-TzFxbiM: Maze picture of the letter M accessed from free site on July 28 2017.

[11] Van der Kolk, p. 56.

[12] Bible Windows: http://biblewindows.com/strongsnum/hebrew/7665.htm Accessed Fall 2016.

[13] Engel, Beverly *It Wasn't Your Fault* New Harbinger Publications Inc., 2015, p. 234.

[14] Yancey's book is published by Zondervan. It is a winner of the Gold Medallion Award and an inspirational bestseller for over twenty years, *Where Is God When it Hurts?* has been revised and updated by the author to explore the many important issues that have arisen during that time. Sensitive and caring, this unique book discusses pain—physical, emotional, and spiritual—and helps us understand why we suffer from it and how to cope with our own and that of others. Using examples from the Bible as well as the author's personal experiences, this expanded edition speaks to everyone for whom life sometimes doesn't make sense. Philip Yancey can help us discover how to reach out to someone in pain even when we don't know what to say. It shows us how we can learn to accept without blame, anger, or fear that which we cannot understand. This info taken from http://www.zondervan.com/where-is-god-when-it-hurts-1 I do recommend this as a good read for all of life's struggling puzzles.

Philip Yancey serves as editor-at-large for *Christianity Today* magazine. He has written thirteen Gold Medallion Award–winning books and won two ECPA Book of the Year awards for *What's So Amazing About Grace?* and *The Jesus I Never Knew.* Four of his books have sold over one million copies. Yancey lives with his wife in Colorado. Website: www.philipyancey.com

[15] *Cyber Hymnal:* http://cyberhymnal.org/htm/h/i/hiseyeis.htm Accessed January 2017. Public domain. The story behind the hymn is "Early in the Spring of 1905, my husband and I were sojourning in Elmira, New York. We contracted a deep friendship for a couple by the name of Mr. and Mrs. Doolittle—true saints of God. Mrs. Doolittle had been bedridden for nigh twenty years. Her husband was an incurable cripple who had to

propel himself to and from his business in a wheelchair. Despite their afflictions, they lived happy Christian lives, bringing inspiration and comfort to all who knew them. One day, while we were visiting with the Doolittles, my husband commented on their bright hopefulness and asked them for the secret of it. Mrs. Doolittle's reply was simple: "His eye is on the sparrow, and I know He watches me." The beauty of this simple expression of boundless faith gripped the hearts and fired the imagination of Dr. Martin and me. The hymn "His Eye Is on the Sparrow" was the outcome of that experience." The next day, she sent the poem to Charles Gabriel who wrote the music.

[16] Bass, Ellen and Davis, Laura. *The Courage to Heal: A Guide for Women Survivors of Child Sexual Abuse* 20th Anniversary Edition. Harper Collins, 2008, p. 188.

[17] *Brainy Quotes*: https://www.brainyquote.com/search_results.html?q=Albert+Einstein Accessed February 1, 2017

[18] Valentine, Erich *Beethoven: A Pictorial Biography* Thames and Hudson, 1958, p. 60

[19] https://www.google.ca/search?q=free+pictures+of+a+sparrow+to+colour&rlz=1C1MSNA_enCA705CA705&tbm=isch&tbo=u&source=univ&sa=X&ved=0ahUKEwj8p-PowazVAhUq0YMKHbZODV4QsAQIQA&biw=1536&bih=686#imgrc=ltVL2aKftW3L_M: Free picture accessed on July 28, 2017

[20] Van der Kolk, p. 281.

[21] Van der Kolk, p. 13.

[22] Van der Kolk p. 235.

[23] Bass and Davis, p. 7.

[24] Van der Kolk, p. 81.

[25] *BBC site:* http://www.bbc.co.uk/religion/religions/judaism/holydays/sabbath.shtml Accessed December 2016

[26] Rowan, Jane *The River of Forgetting* Booksmyth Press, 2010, p. 51.

[27] Greenberg, Pamela *The Complete Psalms: The Book of Prayer Songs in a New Translation* Bloomsbury: New York, 2010, p. 56.

28 West, Kevin *Angel in Aisle 3* Howard Books, 2015, p. 163.

29 *Fear of:* http://www.fearof.net/ Accessed January 2017.

30 Baloche, Paul. Glorious CD, Integrity Music, 2009.

31 *eHow*:http://www.ehow.com/about_5384479_memory-loss-due-trauma.html#ixzz2DXDovgHj From an article entitled **"About Memory Loss Due to Trauma"** by Janet Mulroney Clark, eHow Contributor

32 Van der Kolk, p. 221.

33 Van der Kolk, p. 206.

34 Allender, Dr. Dan B. *The Wounded Heart: Hope for Adult Victims of Childhood Sexual Abuse* Navpress: 2008, p. 38

35 Van der Kolk, p. 212.

36 Rohr, Richard. *Falling Upward; A Spirituality for the two Halves of Life* Jossey Bass, 2011, p. 35.

37 *Bodyresults:*   http://www.bodyresults.com/climbing-everest-training.asp There are many other excellent tips for hiking on this site, as well as others. They can be a reminder that a significant journey takes resources and time. There are even costs for the opportunity to hike the mountain—a license of usually around $10,000 depending where you start the hike. I was struck by one website suggesting you needed a sleeping bag certified to -300 degrees. Count me out on that trip no question! I didn't even know they made such things! I am hoping that was a typo.

38 Allender, p. 14.

39 Van der Kolk, p. 43.

40 Van der Kolk, p. 85.

41 Van der Kolk, p. 70.

42 https://thedivinelamp.wordpress.com/2011/05/14/monday-may-16-pope-john-paul-ii-on-todays-psalm-42-2/   Accessed January 2017.

43 Van der Kolk, p. 21.

44 Van der Kolk, p. 89.

45 Engel, p. 108.

46 http://www.statisticbrain.com/new-years-resolution-statistics/ Accessed October 2016

47 https://www.brainyquote.com/quotes/winston_churchill_131188 Accessed December 7, 2017

48 http://www.lifehack.org/articles/productivity/15-highly-suc-cessful-people-who-failed-their-way-success.html This was a quote from a commencement speech at Harvard. Accessed 2016

49 http://www.goodreads.com/quotes/49588-the-quieter-you-become-the-more-you-can-hear

50 Van der Kolk, p. 45.

51 Van der Kolk, p. 44.

52 http://davidbowmanart.com/eoc/my-child/ My Child: "This piece conveys an intimate, up-close-and-personal feeling of the Savior's love. Notice how all the lines draw your attention and point towards Jesus's face in the center. I chose the name "My Child" because the only thing that could compare (even remotely) to Christ's compassion for us is the love of a parent for his/her child. This image is also intended to put things in perspective. Above all, we are God's children first. He allows us the privilege of experiencing parenthood for ourselves and we are entrusted to be the mothers and fathers of His children here on earth."

53 http://www.dictionary.com/browse/stronghold

54 http://www.biblestudytools.com/commentaries/treasury-of-da-vid/psalms-37-40.html

55 *Bookhaven*: https://bookhaven.stanford.edu/2012/01/martin-luther-king-on-his-day-only-in-the-darkness-can-you-see-the-stars/ Accessed February 1, 2017

56 Sweeting, George *Great Quotes and Illustrations* Word Books, 1985, p. 133.

57 http://www.sermoncentral.com/sermons/a-reverent-psong-lynn-malone-sermon-on-reverence-for-god-194919

58 *Christianity Today*: http://www.christianity.com/church/church-history/timeline/1801-1900/sarah-pollard-didnt-like-her-name-11630530.html Accessed January 2017.

We read the following about Pollard: "Adelaide was named Sarah when she was born in Bloomfield, Iowa on this day, November 27, 1862. She didn't like her given name and adopted Adelaide in its place. Her life was always centered on her faith. After training in Chicago, she taught in several girls' schools and then became active as a Bible teacher, evangelist, and healer. She herself had been healed of diabetes through prayer. Contemporaries saw her as a mystic and saint. During the years that she was unable to go to Africa, she taught at the Christian and Missionary Alliance School in Nyack, New York. Shortly before World War I, she did reach Africa. However, the war forced her to retreat to Scotland. After the fighting was over, she returned to the United States where, despite failing health, she preached in New England. One of her major themes was that Christ would soon return. Adelaide wrote over one hundred other songs, but just how many we do not know for certain, since she seldom signed them, not desiring credit."

[59] Kidner, Derek. *Psalms 1-72, Tyndale Old Testament Commentaries* Intervarsity Press, 1973, p. 130.

[60] *Brainyquotes:* https://www.brainyquote.com/search_results.html?q=Albert+Einstein. Accessed February 3, 2017

[61] Allender. p. 18.

[62] Sweeting, p. 15.

[63] Bass and Davis, p. 46.

[64] This famous book by Charles Dickens is seen on stage and on film prior to Christmas every year. It is a reminder for us not to be "bah humbug" but seek to be examples of compassion. This is done in the life of the main character Scrooge by showing him flashbacks of the past, reminders of the present, and a vision of what could be. They say hindsight is 20-20. Too bad we can't gain that perfect vision in everyday life.

[65] Caine, Christine. *Unstoppable: Running the Race You Were Born to Win.* Zondervan, 2014. Pp 42–43

[66] Van der Kolk, p. 237.

[67] For those much younger than I am, Ann Landers had a column in most newspapers where readers could ask questions about any personal problems (relationships primarily) and she would print her advice.

68 Rowan, p. 244.

69 Facebook entry from www.Likesuccess.com. Accessed February 2017.

70 https://www.workingpreacher.org/preaching.aspx?commentary_id=877

71 Taken from a weekly calendar I had many years ago. A web search led me to Oprah's website, but it was easier to find at: http://www.popsugar.com/smart-living/photo-gallery/35780931/image/35781051/I-know-sure-what-we-dwell-who-we-become

72 Sweeting, p. 64.

73 Willis, John T. and Jones, David G. *The Living Word Commentary on the Old Testament: Psalms* Sweet Publishing Company, 1980, p. 318.

74 http://dailypersonalitydevelopment.com/slow-and-steady-win-the-race/ Accessed December 2016.

75 The five-step model for recovery from grief was first introduced by Swiss psychiatrist Elisabeth Kübler-Ross in her 1969 book, *On Death and Dying.*

For more information about the Me-Too movement please see the following: https://www.washingtonpost.com/news/the-intersect/wp/2017/10/19/the-woman-behind-me-too-knew-the-power-of-the-phrase-when-she-created-it-10-years-ago/?tid=hybrid_collaborative_1_na&utm_term=.49e192a61484

Regarding the discussion of PTSD see the following two links accessed in October 2017:

Link of discussion: http://www.posttraumaticstressinjury.org/

https://operationcompassionatecare.org/historical-names-for-ptsd/

About the Author

MED.

The author of *The Molly Project* has chosen to remain anonymous as a reminder to the reader that it is God and His healing work to be praised. Some anonymity allows you to place yourself in this healing project with better ease.

The author of this book, MED, has been a teacher for many years and has written many musical compositions and some small writing projects, but this is her first book. She drafted the book beginning in 2011 but it wasn't until a fleece project with God (read about Gideon and you will understand one's uncertainty about a new venture) that she took a year off from work to ponder, study, and write. It is her prayer that this be a source of encouragement for those who journey through struggle and provide understanding for those who walk along other's journeys. Blessings to you all as you seek God's healing touch.

Molly and her adult will be available through e-mail and web page, and will also plan some retreats and speaking engagements for ministry to many who suffer.

CPSIA information can be obtained
at www.ICGtesting.com
Printed in the USA
LVHW03s0413040818
585916LV00001B/1/P